Dr. Strangegod

Studies in Comparative Religion
Frederick M. Denny, *Editor*

The Holy Book in Comparative Perspective
Edited by Frederick M. Denny and Rodney L. Taylor

Dr. Strangegod: On the Symbolic Meaning of Nuclear Weapons
By Ira Chernus

Dr. Strangegod

ON THE SYMBOLIC MEANING OF NUCLEAR WEAPONS

Ira Chernus

University of South Carolina Press

Published in Columbia, South Carolina, by the
University of South Carolina Press

FIRST EDITION

Manufactured in the United States of America

Library of Congress Cataloging-in-Publication Data

Chernus, Ira, 1946–
   Dr. Strangegod : on the symbolic meaning of
nuclear weapons.

   (Studies in comparative religion)
   Bibliography: p.
   Includes index.
   1. Nuclear warfare—Religious aspects. I. Title.
II. Title: Doctor Strangegod. III. Series: Studies
in comparative religion (Columbia, S.C.)
BL65.A85C48   1986   291.1'7873   86-11326
ISBN 0-87249-484-5

For Ann

Where there is danger,
That which saves also grows.

Contents

	Acknowledgments	ix
	Introduction: The Symbolic Dimension	3
1.	A Limitless Power	12
2.	The Many Meanings of "Security"	32
3.	Fate and Chance	53
4.	Unreality and Madness	63
5.	Theater of the Absurd	74
6.	The Myth of the Hero	84
7.	The Apocalyptic Vision	91
8.	Sacrifice and Martyrdom	106
9.	Mutual Suicide	119
10.	The Death-Machine as God	133
	Epilogue: Toward the Fourth Level	149
	Notes	169
	Bibliography	176
	Index	182

Acknowledgments

I wish to express my appreciation to a number of people who helped make this book possible. My colleagues in the Department of Religious Studies at the University of Colorado, Boulder, gave unqualified support to my rather unorthodox academic venture, each in his or her own unique and valuable way. The following people read the manuscript at various stages and offered suggestions that were greatly appreciated: David Goldfischer, Ed Linenthal, Marie Cantlon, Denise Straus, Walter Capps, and Gail Maxwell. Ed Linenthal's unflagging and enthusiastic support was especially important to me. Fred Denny, editor of Studies in Comparative Religion, and Ken Scott of the University of South Carolina Press were instrumental in seeing the book come into print. My sincere thanks to all these people. Above all, I want to thank Ann, whose despair and hope inspired this book and brought it into being.

Dr. Strangegod

Introduction

THE SYMBOLIC DIMENSION

One sunny afternoon in early 1944, Captain J. Glenn Gray of the U.S. Army climbed a hill in Italy. At the top of the hill he met the old hermit who lived there. As they sat and talked, watching the battle raging in the valley far below, Gray slowly realized that the hermit had, quite literally, no idea who was shooting at whom, or why. This radically new perspective was, for Glenn Gray, shockingly and profoundly liberating. For as he tried to explain World War II to his hermit friend, he became aware that he himself did not really understand it. "The strangeness of the conflict and my part in it made me shiver," he recollects. "Why were we fighting individuals whom we had never seen and who had never seen us? . . . How did this mad war concern me? For a few minutes I could observe this spectacle through the puzzled eyes of the old hermit, long enough to realize that I understood it as little as he. . . . Some simple and familiar things were seen for the first time in a proper light."[1]

What was this "proper light"? To the hermit there was no discernible difference between the opposing armies. The ideological, political, and economic conflicts that they pointed to as their reasons for waging war were meaningless. The hermit saw only a multitude of human beings, all essentially alike, choosing to inflict violence, and often death, upon each other. And so the hermit might be forgiven for assuming that these human beings actually wanted to engage in mass mayhem—that they found some intrinsic value in the activity itself, apart from any purported aims and

3

purposes. Otherwise their actions would appear totally meaningless and incomprehensible.

But if the hermit could not understand World War II, imagine his bewilderment at the war that followed—the Cold War, with its tens of thousands of nuclear warheads aimed and readied, awaiting only the push of a single button. Imagine that we could join that hermit for a moment and see the nuclear arms race from his perspective. What would we see? Not the "forces of freedom," ready to defend the "free world" against "totalitarian aggression." Nor the "people's armies" standing up against the "imperialist capitalist drive for world domination." These explanations and justifications for nuclear armament would mean nothing to us. We would see, instead, millions of human beings preparing for, or acquiescing in the preparation of, destruction and suffering on a totally unprecedented and unimaginable scale. And we might see some simple and familiar things for the first time in a proper light.

We would see, for example, the essential similarity in the goals, the aspirations, the very humanity of the "freedom-loving" West and the "revolutionary masses" of the East. Although we would see genuine points of difference and dispute, we would also see that these by no means require the production or deployment of nuclear weapons. We might see the behavior of each side leading to its own destruction rather than to fulfillment of its aspirations. And we might ask why the two sides failed to agree on less destructive ways to pursue their rivalry. Thus we would be led to explore again, in a new light, the question: Why nuclear weapons? The answers that dawned upon us would take us beneath all political and ideological concerns. They would show us that the roots of the arms race are buried much deeper than purely rational thinking and planning can reach. We would begin to suspect that nuclear weapons have some innate appeal—that they whisper seductively to some essentially human element hidden in the psyches of us all. So we would begin to search for the intrinsic value that all human beings might find in perpetuating nuclear confrontation as an end in itself. Finally, like Glenn Gray, we would ask ourselves, "How does this mad war concern me?" And we would have to admit that there is much we do not yet understand.

Complete understanding is, of course, an elusive and probably impossible goal. Those who spend their working days trying to unravel the enigma we call "human being" tend nowadays to concentrate on very narrow and specialized perspectives. Thus I offer the following reflections on the question "Why nuclear weapons?" in full awareness that I speak out of my own partial perspective, that of a specialist in comparative religion (though I have drawn freely from a wide variety of other fields). If there is value in these thoughts, it is the value of one piece in a large and complex puzzle.

Combining my professional perspective with the hermit's perspective, I ask here whether people find some intrinsic value in possessing nuclear weapons that is more fundamental than the normally accepted justifications for nuclear armament. The hermit's perspective makes an affirmative answer at least plausible. The perspective of academic religious studies makes it even more plausible, for in religious studies we often find that people may not understand the full meaning and motivation of their own behavior. Perhaps all of us are drawn, in some degree, to possessing and even using nuclear weapons, despite our vigorous denials of this possibility.

The key to understanding hidden meanings and motivations in religion—and in the nuclear age—lies in the interpretation of symbols. In the chapters that follow, I shall pursue three basic hypotheses:

1. Nuclear weapons have a number of complex and highly significant symbolic meanings in our culture.

2. These meanings are often similar to those of traditional religious symbols; thus the Bomb can and should be studied in much the same way that academic specialists study religious symbolism.

3. Through this approach we discover that symbolic meanings make nuclear weapons more acceptable, appealing, fascinating, and perhaps even indispensable to us, although this process remains largely unconscious most of the time.

Those who hope that humanity will soon eliminate its nuclear arsenals may find little encouragement in the body of this book—

except for the encouragement that comes from seeing the previously obscured roots of a stubborn problem. In the epilogue, however, I shall suggest that my analysis may yield seeds that can bear the fruits of hope.

Before proceeding to the discussion of the Bomb and religious symbolism, it may be useful to offer some comments on the nature of symbolism in general. The notion of "symbol" in modern thought is highly complex, and its meaning is often hotly debated. For the present purposes, though, a simple understanding of symbolism will suffice. A symbol is a concrete representation of some intangible reality. Thus symbols are particularly crucial in religion, for the reality of which religion wants to speak is notoriously intangible. The symbol, then, is a sort of container for that which we understand to be "uncontainable"; therefore we know that every symbol is doomed from the start to be inadequate. Yet the symbol is all we have. So we use words like *beautiful* and *devilish*, and actions such as the kiss or the raised middle finger, and images like the American eagle holding arrows and olive branch. The symbol, being word or action or image, builds a bridge between ourselves, with our limited abilities to conceive and understand, and that which by its nature transcends those limited abilities.

A symbol may be distinguished from a sign. A sign is simply a substitute for some reality that we can grasp fully without the sign. A stop sign, for example, contains nothing beyond the simple and fully understood command to stop. The number 2 is a sign for the fully comprehended concept of two entities taken together. But a kiss or the word *beautiful* is by its very nature elusive; we can articulate only a part of its meaning in word and thought. Its full meaning can be communicated only through itself; it is not a substitute for anything else. Thus no one person at one time can grasp all the meanings of the symbol; in practical terms (if not in principle) its meaning is infinite. This means, among other things, that the symbol is able to communicate contradictory meanings simultaneously. When we call a child "devilish," we are usually communicating a wide range of both negative and positive meanings simultaneously. The eagle that proffers both arrows and olive branch together certainly does so. In fact, most of the truly powerful symbols in human history, both religious and nonreligious, have gained their power from their ability to communicate contradictory meanings simultaneously. All of these great symbols share one common message: at its most profound level, our understanding of reality must be paradoxical. Thus a sign must accept the law of noncontradiction; it must say either *A* or *not-A*, but not both. A symbol, however, is free from this law, and so is human life at its most meaningful levels.

We have learned much during this century about the crucial role that symbols and signs play in our lives. It is now commonplace in many academic discussions to assume that human beings are essentially sign and symbol creators and manipulators; this is what marks us off from the other animals. Language itself is the most obvious example that signs are indispensable. Nor could we live without physical gestures, pictures, numbers, and the like, whose meanings are immediately obvious. But symbols play a special role in human life, for when we deal with the "big picture"—with life and death, meaning and purpose, joy and suffering at their most intense—it is our symbols that both guide us to and express for us our most genuine responses.

In these deepest and most profound moments of life, we often find that our responses are highly ambivalent and sometimes contradictory; the symbol is especially crucial here because of its capacity to express different and even opposed meanings simultaneously. But the symbol can do more than this: it can also show us the relationship among these apparently contradictory meanings and fit them together to form a unified whole. Thus it gives us access to direct experience of that deeper dimension of life in which opposites can merge to reflect a larger unity. To put it simply, life "hangs together" and makes sense to us, if it does at all, only because we have symbols to make sense out of it. Symbols are the bridge that puts us in touch with those basic realities often called into question at life's most critical moments; without such a bridge, we would be cut off in our time of greatest need.

Where do symbols come from? The psychologists tell us that they come from the unconscious; the sociologists and anthropologists tell us that they come from our culture. Both are right. While symbols may be best understood as originating and functioning largely on the unconscious level, where the law of noncontradiction is not especially honored, few if any of us will have the privilege of "inventing" a symbol. The vast majority of our symbols and their meanings are an inheritance that we receive at birth from the generations that preceded us. It might be said with some justice that "to grow up" means to learn the symbols of one's culture and their many-sided meanings. If we cannot master our culture's symbols at some level at least, we probably cannot become human in any meaningful sense. Thus both an individual's sense of identity and a culture's sense of identity are built upon the building blocks of its fundamental symbols.

In most cultures in human history, the basic building blocks were what we today call religious symbols. Both the individual and the society gained a sense of meaning in life because they saw themselves in meaningful relation to fundamental yet intangible cosmic realities, which were mediated through the symbols. And because the culture's symbols were at least ideally related to each other in a coherent network of interlocking meanings, individuals could be convinced that in some (perhaps inscrutable) way reality itself held together in a coherent and therefore meaningful fashion. In traditional Western civilization, this coherence of reality was assured because all religious symbols were held together by one central and omnipresent symbol: God.

Indeed, the Western experience of God—whether it be Yahweh, Zeus, God the Father, Jupiter, Thor, or Allah—reflects the same basic pattern exhibited in most religious symbolism. Modern students of religion have found that religious symbols frequently (some would say always) mediate a reality that seems to be infinite—unlimited in power, in knowledge, in space, and in time. This reality transcends rational comprehension; it seems to be alien, inscrutable, and unpredictable. Such a sense of irrational "otherness" is awesome and terrifying; often it is closely linked to the threat of death. Simultaneously, though, the religious symbol represents coherence, structure, and order in the world. It beckons with its assurance of all-embracing security. In this sense, it is related to the promise of continuing life. So religious symbols are paradoxical. They tell us that when we reach life's depths and extremities, order and disorder—the rational and the irrational, life and death—meet in the unifying embrace of a limitless power. Hence they tell us that to gain order and life we must accept, and perhaps experience intensely, disorder and death. The two are two sides of a single coin. This phenomenology of the religious symbol will serve as our basic schema for interpreting the symbolism of the Bomb.

Because the meaning of a symbol is necessarily open-ended, it would be impossible for any single analysis to exhaust the symbolic meanings of nuclear weapons. One might say that the apparently endless number of meanings plausibly posited for these weapons is in itself confirmation of their function as symbol. So no writer can confidently claim to present an all-inclusive survey—much less the single correct interpretation—of the meaning of nuclear weapons in our culture. In the chapters that follow, therefore, I hope only to outline some of the symbolic meanings of nuclear weapons. I shall be more than happy if other writers come along to present different analyses and different views; I see this book as a first word on the subject, certainly not the last word. Many such attempts will be needed before we begin to grasp the complexities of the subject. At this point the crucial task is not to achieve irrefutable conclusions but simply to open up a new perspective on the subject. Whether we call it the symbolic perspective or the hermit's perspective, it is a wider perspective that can take us out of the rut of repetitive political and ethical analyses that seem to lock us more tightly into the status quo. Participation in the process of interpretation may be more important and more liberating than rigid insistence on the validity of our findings.

Several criticisms of this book can already be anticipated. Some may argue that it is the nation as a whole, not merely its Bomb, that has taken the place of the traditional figure of God. There is merit in this argument, and it would serve us well to have it vigorously pursued. But I believe that by now nuclear powers can no longer distinguish between the nation and its Bomb; the Bomb is itself the overwhelming symbol of national power and prestige. This is evident in the determination of nations like France, Brazil, Argentina, and South Africa to develop their own nuclear-weapons programs. The benefits these countries can gain from such huge expenditures are almost entirely symbolic—and for that reason all the more alluring and indispensable. Nowhere else but in the Bomb can the many abstract and intangible meanings of nationalism be made concrete. In that sense it is a striking analogue to the very concrete images of God at the center of the Western religions. Nowhere is this convergence of nationalism and nuclear armament more apparent than in the Soviet Union. Many analyses suggest that the Soviets' immense expenditures to keep up in the arms race are dangerously weakening that country's economy (and some suggest that the huge American investment in weaponry is designed to keep the Soviets in this self-defeating spiral). But the Soviets insist on pursuing this course largely, I believe, because they know that only their nuclear arsenal entitles them to the status of "superpower." Apparently the symbolic significance of that status outweighs all other considerations.

This brings us to the larger question "What about the Russians?" which might also be raised as a criticism of this book. My illustrations and analyses of particulars are virtually all drawn from the American political and cultural experience, for one reason alone: the United States is the only country I can claim to understand even minimally. I would be very pleased if someone with sufficient knowledge of the Russian language, culture, and political scene could write a companion volume covering the same themes from the Soviet Union's perspective. The specific interpretations of nuclear symbolism would be strikingly different, no doubt. But I suspect that general lines of thinking and the general conclusions would turn out to be much the same. The European part of the U.S.S.R., which is the politically and culturally dominant part, is historically just as much part of the Christian West as is the United States. And many of the symbolic patterns we shall examine may well be universal responses to universal human needs and desires. (I would add, too, that the question "What about the Russians?" is used all too frequently in the United States to avoid asking the more painful question, "What about the Americans?")

A third criticism that might arise is that some of the interpretations advanced here seem to contradict each other. That is true, but it is actually a positive point in favor of the thesis that nuclear weapons do function as symbols for us. Any treatment of the nuclear issue must deal with the many contradictions in United

States public policy and American communal and individual attitudes. The most compelling explanation, to my mind, lies in the symbolic dimension of these weapons. Nuclear symbolism, like all religious symbolism, must embrace a wide variety of contradictions and paradoxes. Any writer who hopes to do justice to the subject must therefore appear to be self-contradictory. Indeed, it may turn out that the more contradictory their symbolic meanings, the more appealing the weapons are.

But one basic theme will appear clearly throughout all the complex twists and turns of this study: nuclear weapons are appealing to us because of their many symbolic meanings, and so we are reluctant to part with them. Shall we ever part with them, or shall we cling to them as faithful adherents until the day that they dispose of us? No one can say, and this book makes no predictions. It does predict, however, that no movement for nuclear disarmament can succeed with purely rational arguments and political methods. We shall never be able to turn away from our nuclear faith until we first understand it in its own symbolic terms. Above all, we must understand that, just as our ancestors found all religious meanings converging in one awesome beloved God, so we find all religious meanings converging in our strange yet alluring God—the Bomb.

1

A LIMITLESS POWER

Amid all the controversy about nuclear weapons, there is one proposition on which everyone can agree: the explosion of a nuclear weapon is an awesome event. Those who have witnessed one can hardly find words to express their feelings; an official government report of the first nuclear explosion (a small one by today's standards) called it "magnificent, beautiful, stupendous, and terrifying .... Words are inadequate tools. ... It had to be witnessed to be realized."[1] The idea of nuclear destruction can inspire equal awe in the common person who has never witnessed it firsthand; one student wrote: "That the possibility for such large-scale destruction of the gift of life exists . . . fills me with awe and a chilling sense of dread."[2]

These concepts of awe, dread, terror, and stupendous magnificence, which recur in so many reactions to nuclear explosions, signal students of religion that the basic concepts with which they work are relevant here. The modern academic study of religion was founded in large part on Rudolf Otto's claim that these emotions lie at the heart of all religious experience. Otto, in his book *The Idea of the Holy*, challenged the prevailing view that religion is basically a matter of beliefs and morals. Rather, he suggested, religion is essentially concerned with a unique kind of experience, which he labeled the experience of the holy or (almost synonymously) the "numinous." A sense of awe, of fear and trembling, is always part of this multifaceted experience: "Here we have a terror fraught with an inward shuddering .... English has the words 'awe', 'aweful', which in their deeper and most special sense approximate closely to our meaning. . . . It first begins to stir in the feeling of 'something uncanny', 'eerie', or 'weird'. It is this feeling which, emerging in the mind of primeval man, forms the starting-point for the entire religious development in history. 'Daemons' and 'gods' alike spring from this root."[3]

In analyzing this phenomenon, Otto immediately adds: "It will be felt at once that there is yet a further element which must be added, that, namely, of 'might', 'power', 'absolute overpowering-ness'."[4] Another founding figure in modern religious studies, Gerardus van der Leeuw, has gone even further and suggested that in all religious experiences "power" is the crucial and essential element, and thus he posits "power" as the key notion in the understanding of religion. And, following Otto, he suggests that *awe* is the best word to describe our response to religious experiences of power. A third major religious thinker of the twentieth century, Paul Tillich, has put the sense of infinitude or unlimited-ness in the central place in defining and interpreting religion. If we combine the views of these men, we can say that religion always involves the sense of the numinous, which is evoked by an experience of unlimited power. We begin to see, then, that it may be reasonable to suggest that nuclear weapons have some role akin to the religious in today's world.

The awesome terror of a nuclear explosion comes, of course, from its awesome destructiveness. However, few people have any accurate sense of just how much damage a nuclear explosion can do. Rather, this sense of destruction is expressed in vague but very familiar words: "We might blow the world up," or "the end of civilization as we know it," or "the end of life on the planet."

These expressions and others like them are attempts to articulate a sense of widespread or even total devastation that cannot be expressed in literal terms. They themselves, then, are symbols; but it seems more precise to say that they are verbal equivalents for that sense of annihilation of which "the Bomb" itself is our dominant (and in some cases exclusive) symbol. Our fear is a response not only to our conscious understanding of what such a weapon can do, but also to our unconscious anxieties. Franco Fornari writes: "The most cursory study of dream life and of the phantasies of the insane shows that ideas of world-destruction . . . are latent in the unconscious mind. And since the atomic bomb is less a weapon of war than a weapon of extermination . . . the first promise of the atomic age is that it can make some of our nightmares come true."[5] As a symbol that can unite the conscious and unconscious levels, the Bomb thus fuses our real fears and our fantasy fears into a single whole.

Yet awe involves more than just terror, and the awesomeness of nuclear weapons reflects more than just their power to destroy. A nuclear blast in the desert or ocean, or underground, can inspire numinous awe, even when there is no apparent destruction. Anyone who has lived in Las Vegas, Nevada, can attest to this. It is not unusual there to feel the earth shaking, as if from a small earthquake, when a bomb explodes underground 120 miles away. Nothing of value has been destroyed, yet there is, for many people, a strange feeling of uneasiness, of the "uncanny." There is something eerie in the thought of power so great that it is virtually unlimited. And, in fact, nuclear scientists assert that the power of their weapons is limited only by their supposed military practicality. In theory there is no limit to the potential energy that could be released by a nuclear explosion. The very existence of a bomb with unlimited power poses a threat to our sense of normalcy. The first nuclear explosion was described as "weird, incredible, somehow disturbing. . . . One senses the foundations of one's own universe trembling."[6] If such weapons can be made, then perhaps anything can happen.

This brings us to the second aspect of the numinous: the sense of weirdness and eeriness comes not only from awesome power and terror but also from the aspect of mystery that is inevitably part of every religious experience. To encounter the numinous is necessarily to encounter that which is in principle beyond all explanation. It is mysterious not only because it transcends every horizon that human understanding might ever attain, but also because it seems to be "wholly other" than anything the mind has ever understood or might ever hope to understand. Its character is wholly incommensurable with the realm of human comprehension. All we can do is recoil in frozen wonder. Thus, as Norman Moss asserts, the fear of nuclear destruction "is not a localized one, but a general fear of what can be done, the kind of fear that men once had of God."[7] The Bomb, in short, is a symbol not only of annihilation but also of power without limit—of omnipotence—and hence of numinous mystery.

Omnipotence is always related to mystery, but in the case of the Bomb this relationship takes a special shape. Nuclear weapons were possible only because of the pioneering pure research of Albert Einstein, Niels Bohr, Enrico Fermi, and others, men who originally had no interest in creating weapons but, rather, sought to "unlock the secrets of the universe," "to understand the basic building-blocks of the physical world." And these weapons are special in that they rely not on some particular chemical or physical principles, but on the basic principle that underlies our entire conception of material reality in the twentieth century—the structure of the atom. The mystery embodied in the Bomb is the mystery of reality itself, and it is the nuclear scientists who have "unlocked" and "harnessed" it.

It is little wonder that, after the first atomic explosions, "people were willing and anxious to listen to anything an atomic scientist had to say. In the public mind, these men had something of the aura of magicians; they seemed to possess power," in the words of Moss.[8] There is little reason to believe that things have changed much in this regard, for the atomic scientist is still, like the priests and shamans of earlier times, privileged to explore, understand, and (most importantly) manipulate the very power by which the universe was created. If "nuclear weapons have come to be imbued with an almost mystic quality,"[9] it is largely because they symbolize an ability to control and play with a power that once was reserved for God alone—the power of creation. The particular phrases we use are very important; we say that we have "unlocked the secret of the atom." This implies that the atom itself, like God, has held this secret mystery, this deepest of all wisdom, from the very beginning. But only in the twentieth century have human beings become privy to it.

It is not surprising, then, that there has been such extreme concern, perhaps one might say paranoia, about preserving the "secret" of nuclear weaponry. As Robert Lifton suggests, behind

the political reasons offered for this secrecy is a deeper psychological concern, a "mystique around keeping hidden and exclusive
one's relationship to ultimate destructive power. . . . To hold on to
the secret is to hold on to life itself."[10] Lifton relates this to the
child's sense that knowledge about one's personal origin is a
(sexual) secret. Compounding this psychological truth, however, is
the scientifically verifiable truth that we have penetrated to the
secret of our cosmological origin as well. We are, in a sense,
possessors of an absolute wisdom, what was once called divine
wisdom, and we feel compelled to prevent others from obtaining it.
Hence the preoccupation of the 1950s with the problem of atomic
spies. Of course, by now it is clear to us that this wisdom cannot be
the possession of any single nation; yet as a human race we still
sense that we have, for the first time, been made privy to the secret
mysteries of the cosmos, and we still must see our nuclear scientists
as wizards. With few exceptions, the scientists play the role we
would have them play and reinforce our assumption that they do
have magical wisdom. And the sense of social responsibility, even
guilt, that earlier nuclear scientists felt seems to be disappearing,
perhaps because the scientists have become, in Moss's title, "Men
Who Play God."

There are, throughout the world, ancient mythologies that tell us
that divine wisdom is accessible only to the dead. Psychologist
James Hillman says: "The thick walls thrown up against death
attest to its power and our need . . . . the urge towards the
fundamental truth of life. If some call this truth God, then the
impulse towards death is also towards meeting with God, which
some theologies hold is possible only by death."[11] Perhaps it is
more than coincidence that those same scientists who "unlocked
the secrets of creation" have also unlocked the secret of death on a
massive and previously unimaginable scale.

Yet the mystery of the Bomb is so great that many may doubt
whether any scientist can fully comprehend it. The ancient priest
knew that he served a power that was ultimately beyond human
comprehension, and thus beyond concepts and words. Otto tells us
that the best word to describe the religious response to numinous
mystery is *stupor*. "Stupor . . . signifies blank wonder, an astonish-
ment that strikes us dumb, amazement absolute."[12] Robert Lifton

found the same feeling among the *hibakusha*, survivors of the Hiroshima bombing: "Ultimately, the ineffability of atomic bomb exposure—its relationship to cosmic mysteries that one can neither grasp nor explain—gives *hibakusha* an inner sense that *all* talk about it is inauthentic. . . . As the downtrodden woman laborer tells us: 'It was beyond words.' "[13] True wisdom, true understanding of the secrets of the cosmos thus lies ultimately with the Bomb itself, and only by extension with those who have understood the Bomb to some extent.

Nuclear weapons, then, are a powerful symbol of both omnipotence and omniscience, the power and wisdom and mystery at the source of creation. In both these respects, the Bomb has those attributes that have traditionally been ascribed to the God of the Western religions; these are accompanied by a third—omnipresence—which is also characteristic of nuclear weapons. Their effect is everywhere and inescapable. This was most vividly portrayed, perhaps, in the popular novel and film *On the Beach*, which depicts fallout from a northern-hemisphere war creeping south and ultimately destroying all life on the planet. There is no escape; one can only await the inexorable although invisible death that is steadily approaching. Here, as with so many other topics we shall discuss, it is beside the point to ask whether this image is scientifically valid. The essential point is that the image accurately reflects what is commonly believed about nuclear weapons, and therefore it reflects the symbolic truth that shapes our perception of reality. Moreover the same sense of pervasive, inescapable death is at work in our perception of undetonated nuclear weapons. Sitting in their silos or on their submarines, they are still representations of omnipresent annihilating power.

The thousands of nuclear weapons that are linked together by the interlocking communications networks of the military do indeed form, in the public mind and in reality, one single bomb, one single gigantic power whose effects are everywhere. Thus, when we speak of "the Bomb," we express most directly our sense of this attribute of omnipresence. But because this threat is everywhere, it is not locatable; it is in fact nowhere in particular, and therefore it becomes an invisible yet omnipresent reality.[14] It may be relevant to note here that Lifton, in studying survivors of Hiroshima, was

struck in particular by their sense of contagion; even those who had
escaped the effects of the bomb feared contact with those who had
been affected, because "there was the feeling that deadly
castastrophe knew no limits . . . . a sense of individual powerlessness in the face of an invisible, all-enveloping, and highly mysterious poison."[15] For our purposes it is particularly significant that
Lifton immediately goes on to note "the inner sense that this *total*
contamination—seemingly limitless in time and space—must have
a supernatural, or at least more-than-natural origin, so that one's
survival was likely to be merely a temporary respite from these
invisible forces."[16]

Yet at the same time we must admit that until recently very few
people have been visibly disturbed by the omnipresence of nuclear
weapons. There are many reasons for this apparent unconcern; one
is particularly relevant here. Jerome D. Frank speaks of that
bio-psychological characteristic of humans which he calls "insen-
sitivity to the remote . . . . We have no biological need to detect and
respond to stimuli that do not impinge on any sense organ. . . . 'Out
of sight, out of mind' operates with respect to modern weapons."[17]
In other words, we do not respond to nuclear weapons because they
are "nowhere in particular" and in that sense are invisible. Historians of religion have described an analogous phenomenon, which
they call the "Deus Otiosus,' the god who is otiose (i.e., distant,
removed from immediate human concerns). Typically the otiose
god is the creator god, the god who is said to have brought the
universe into being and then retired to his home in the sky. While
this god is not an object of regular worship, there is often a
tendency to resort to him in times of particular trouble, when the
other gods seem ineffectual. In such emergencies, he is asked to
come down from the sky to protect, defend, or rescue his people
from some danger.

It may well be that nuclear weapons have become the Deus
Otiosus of contemporary culture. The otiose god is the hidden god,
the god who remains unrevealed to the living. It is often only
through death that one can make contact with this god and bring
him out of his hiddenness. Perhaps, then, the hidden Bomb beckons
to us today as did the otiose god of an earlier age.

The gods, the sacred, the numinous do beckon to us. Their

unlimited power, mystery, and inscrutable wisdom make them objects of awe and dread, but this is only one side of the picture. There is always a simultaneous attraction to the holy, for it inspires fascination as well as fear. This fascination may rise to a level of enchantment, intoxication, or even Dionysian ecstasy. As the fear stems largely from the sense of unlimitedness, our inability to control or even predict the ways of unlimited power, so equally does the fascination stem from this same quality. For only that which is unlimited can promise unlimited good, help, salvation. The blessedness it offers cannot be put into words, but it is sensed as a positive gift beyond compare. Just because it is ineffable, it seems to be a bliss beyond all limits—the peace that passes understanding.

Just as all can agree that nuclear explosions are awesome, so it is hard to contest the assertion that there is a fascinating aspect in them. And just as the religious person is drawn to the numinous, wanting to identify with it and merge with its power, so we may be drawn to the Bomb. Survivors of the Hiroshima nuclear bombing reacted in part with this kind of fascination: "For some, identification with the bomb was related to being in awe of its power. The grocer, for instance . . . remembered feeling 'only the greatness of the bomb.' . . . This combination of awe and fear could sometimes come close to admiration."[18] But Americans who have not lived through such an experience can show similar responses when asked about nuclear weapons: "Many people, in fact, used 'fascination' to describe a significant part of their response, now and then: 'Just the tremendous power of the thing,' said the poet from Philadelphia, 'and the sort of slow cloud going up and the incredible colors of the blast and just the huge majesty' would never be forgotten."[19] Perhaps the most important aspect of nuclear weapons as symbol is this simultaneous response of dread and fascination, which draws us toward the Bomb at the very same moment that we flee from it.

We are always fascinated by mystery, but the fascination is especially strong when the mystery is bound up with explosive manifestations of power, and the greater the intensity, the greater the attraction (and repulsion too). The tremendous public attention focused on the Mount St. Helens volcanic eruption is evidence of this. It was hardly due to the loss of life and injury; people simply could not help wanting to see a mountain blow up. Nor can we avoid being fascinated when anything blows up, from an oil refinery to the fireworks on the Fourth of July. If we can understand this fascination with explosive power, we can understand something of the complexity surrounding nuclear weapons as a symbol.

What happens when we witness a manifestation of intense power? It commands and demands our full attention. This may be most obvious in the case of an explosion, but it is equally true when we see a powerful waterfall or a powerful runner or a powerful film. It "takes our breath away," it "rivets us to the spot," perhaps it even "blows our mind." For a brief moment, our normal state of distractedness, of fragmented and scattered attention, is suspended, and all of our mental, emotional, and physical energies are concentrated on a single object. It is, in a sense, an involuntary entry into something like the meditative state that yogins attain by consciously concentrating all of their energies on a single object. Such a moment forces all of our normally scattered and conflicting faculties to work together in harmony, all focusing on a common object and therefore binding themselves together. And, quite simply, it feels good.

But we do more than observe power; at the same time we enter into a relation with it. Having focused our energies, we find that somehow those energies have gone out to get in closer touch with the power, and the powerful reality seems to have come closer to us. Therefore we find an inner feeling of power rising to resonate with the power outside us. Watching a powerful runner, we come closer to feeling what it would be like to run powerfully ourselves. Hearing a powerful singer, we come closer to feeling what it would be like to sing powerfully. And witnessing an explosion, we come closer to feeling what it would be like to explode. Experiencing external power, we also experience internal power, and we feel more powerful, more vital, more alive. Many interpreters of modern culture have suggested that it is just this feeling of vitality, of aliveness, which is most fundamentally missing, most desperately sought after, in our world today. Some have interpreted the modern preoccupation with sexuality, with technology, with drugs, with sports, with various forms of violence, as so many ways of experiencing vitality and power.

But why explosions? Isn't it somehow perverse to be fascinated by destruction, to look to it as a source of personal enhancement? It is important to recall Otto's approach here. He was consciously superseding a view of religion that saw it necessarily linked with morality. The religious experience, Otto claimed, is amoral; that is, moral considerations do not enter into it. It may be associated with phenomena that are called either moral or immoral, but in itself it is ethically neutral. And it is always ambivalent. It always inspires fear, as any destructive explosion will, but it also inspires a fascination that finds moral evaluation irrelevant. Praise or blame may well be appropriate later, but first one must understand. If we always feel the external power as if it existed within ourselves, the question becomes: Why do we feel attracted to, as well as repelled by, the experience of exploding?

There is a school of thought that would answer this question in purely sexual terms. This approach does contain some truth. Certainly we cannot experience an explosion without responding to some extent in sexual terms, feeling it as an analogue to orgasm. Some would suggest that the explosive destruction of war itself is a sublimation of sexual energy: "Through war, then, society allows the individuals to experience the destructive orgasm which usually cannot be reached on the individual level," says Fornari.[20] For such theorists, it might be quite important to note that nuclear-war strategists speak of the possibility of a "spasm war," a sudden outburst of total and uncontrolled nuclear destruction.

But the explosion of orgasm is itself only one instance of a broader category of experience, which we might call "release" or "transcendence." Orgasm is desired (beyond its purely physical pleasure) because it allows us to be released, if only for a brief instant, from our everyday world, from our ordinary reality, from ourselves. It allows us to explode those limits that define world and self. Every explosion is a symbol of the destruction of limits, and this symbolic dimension, rather than the merely sexual dimension, is the key to understanding our fascination with explosive power. In order to live we need structure, differentiation, and orientation in space and time, a sense of distinction between "me" and "not-me."

But, as anthropologist Victor Turner has argued, that structure becomes stricture; it binds us and weighs us down so that eventually we feel it as a burden, albeit a necessary one.

While we fear the loss of structure and self, we also want to be free of them. We would like to transcend the limits that these structures place upon us, although to do so would mean to lose our sense of "normalcy," of "sanity," of "self." Thus societies develop structured means by which they can experience temporary releases from structure. Sexuality is one of these; in most societies religious ritual is another means, because the sacred, as we have noted, is marked by unlimited power. To stand in relation to the sacred is to experience the transcendence of limits—ultimate powerfulness. One of the crucial effects of secularization may well be the loss of ritualized moments of release from structure, the loss of socially sanctioned experiences of contact with, and absorption in, unlimited power. Modern culture has invented new means for gaining this kind of transcendence, means that have become highly controversial in our society. Again, sexuality is inevitably chief among them, while drugs, music of abandon, and acts of violence must also be included here.

The controversy surrounding these means of transcendence seems to indicate that many in our society fear such experiences of release, finding them threatening. This fear may indicate a repressed desire for release, one that is so overwhelming that individuals must totally banish the possibility both for themselves and for others. Yet human history indicates that the desire for experiences of transcendence will not go away; it will merely take new forms. For the aspiration to transcendence of limits is an aspiration to sacrality; it is, in traditional Western terms, an aspiration to the imitation of God. Perhaps, then, it is more than coincidental that opposition to these new forms of transcendence comes from political quarters that have most avidly supported the development and deployment of weapons of war: in war we find a form of transcendence that may be more intense than any of the other forms discussed here.

Glenn Gray, reflecting on his experiences in World War II, suggests that the major appeal of war for most soldiers comes from the fascination that manifestations of power and magnitude hold for the human spirit. Some scenes of battle . . . are able to overawe the single individual and hold him in a spell. He is lost in their majesty. His ego temporarily deserts him, and he is absorbed in what he sees. An awareness of power that far surpasses his limited imagination transports him into a state of mind unknown in his everyday experience. . . . The awe that steals over us at such times is not essentially a feeling of triumph, but, on the contrary, a recognition of power and grandeur to which we are subject. There is not so much a separation of the self from the world as a subordination of the self to it.[21]

These characteristics of war would, of course, be infinitely intensified in a nuclear war, as Gray points out: "If ever the world is blown to bits by some superbomb, there will be those who will watch the spectacle to the last minute, without fear, disinterestedly, and with detachment. . . . The self is no longer important to the observer; it is absorbed into the objects with which it is concerned."[22]

Lifton found the very same phenomenon among *hibakusha.* Citing the memory of one survivor—"I lost myself and was carried away"—Lifton comments, "The phrase he and others used, *muga-muchu,* literally 'without self, without a center,' suggests an obliteration of the boundaries of the self."[23] In a nuclear explosion all limits are surpassed and all structure abolished, as the victims are returned to a state of primal chaos. And so nuclear weapons "may be psychically perceived as the most Dionysian stimulants of all. . . . Total annihilation may then become a desirable, even joyous possibility."[24] Anyone who has seen the film *Dr. Strangelove,* with its concluding orgiastic mushroom-cloud montage, will have a vivid impression of the Dionysian dimension of nuclear destruction. In the nuclear age, the mushroom cloud has become our most vivid symbol of the *"big whoosh"*—the total annihilation of structure and the permanent release from self.

It is not only the individual but also the society as a whole that hopes to gain power from experiences of destruction. Roger Caillois suggests that this was the function of the orgiastic festival in traditional cultures, and that today war has taken the place of the festival:

> All excesses are permitted, for society expects to be regenerated as a result of excesses, waste, orgies, and violence. It hopes for new vigor to come out of explosion and exhaustion. . . . From everywhere the long-inhibited joy of destruction springs forth, the pleasure of leaving an object shapeless and unrecognizable. . . . It introduces man to an intoxicating world in which the presence of death makes him shiver and confers a superior value upon his various actions. He believes that he will acquire a psychic vigor—just as through the descent to the inferno in ancient initiations—out of proportion to mundane experiences. . . . When war loses all moderation, mobilizes the energies of a people, expends, without counting, the resources of a great nation, when it violates every rule and every law, when it has ceased even in part to resemble anything human—it is then that war appears to wear the most luminous halo. . . . Dedicated to wastefulness and capable of engulfing whatever has form and identity, war results in a dual and sumptuous release for life that is tired of petty prohibitions and prudent refinements. A monstrous societal brew and climax of existence, a time of sacrifice but also of violation of every rule, a time of mortal peril but yet sanctifying, a time of abnegation and also of license—war has every right to take the place of the festival in the modern world and to excite the same fascination and fervor. It is inhuman, and it is sufficient to be deemed divine.[25]

Glenn Gray's observations in World War II seem to bear out Caillois's argument. He too finds that "war compresses the greatest opposites into the smallest space and the shortest time."[26] "The soldier-killer is learning to serve a different deity, and his concern is with death and not life, destruction and not construction. . . . The delight in destroying has . . . an ecstatic character."[27] It is hardly surprising to hear a similar stress on societal disorder among *hibakusha* remembering the bombing of Hiroshima: "During peacetime, in ordinary life, men are restricted by social codes and tradition, but in war they are freed from such social restrictions. So that those who experience war know what man really is and what he can do. They may return with a realization that man can do almost anything."[28]

Lifton found this remark typical of a widespread feeling: "Related to the sense of death in life was a total disruption of individual and social order—of rules governing what is expected of one and whom one can depend on."[29] This absence of societal order reflected an absence of any natural order at all: "The decimation of the city created an atmosphere so permeated by bizarre evidence of death as to make whatever life remained seem unrelated to a 'natural order'. . . . Most 'unnatural' of all was the sudden nonexistence of the city itself—as described by the history professor: 'I saw that Hiroshima had disappeared. . . . What I felt then and still feel now I just can't explain with words. . . . But Hiroshima didn't exist—that was mainly what I saw—Hiroshima just didn't exist.' "[30] The same professor expressed the fundamental point of our discussion in the most succinct possible way: "Such a weapon has the power to make everything into nothing."[31]

But religious mythology indicates that the fascination with destruction and annihilation goes beyond a hidden desire for personal and societal release. In virtually every culture known to us, we find a myth of creation that speaks of a primordial chaos, which existed "in the beginning." It seems likely that even the Bible, if properly understood, begins with a creation imposed on a preexisting chaos. And in most cultures there is some sort of ritual, often a festival, which evokes the experience of this chaos so that the transition from the void to creation can be reenacted. The most influential interpretation of this myth and ritual pattern has been offered by Mircea Eliade. He suggests that it offers a cosmic analogue to the release from structure on the individual and societal levels. The escape from the burdens of differentiation is immensely enhanced by the belief that all differentiations everywhere in the universe have been erased. Only in such a state of formless "coincidence of opposites" can all limits be transcended; only in such a state can there be full omnipotence, omniscience, omnipresence, and, most importantly in Eliade's view, eternity.

At the center of this theory is the claim that human beings find endless change unendurable. The passage of time robs reality of its vitality, power, and structure. In the temporal perspective, all things are running down, heading toward dissolution. Religion is fundamentally concerned with transcending the limitations of time. But time is a function of differentiation. Only because there is a difference between this and that, between me and not-me, can there be interaction between distinct realities, and only because of such interaction can we be aware of the passage of time. In an isolation tank, time is a meaningless concept, and so it is in the undifferentiated state of primal chaos. So, by returning to the time of the beginning, religious people hope to experience the annulment of time. History seems to be wiped away, and the reality of change is denied. Because that moment of beginnings is always available in myth and ritual, it represents a permanent, eternal reality.

Secularization, in removing many of our symbols of power, has simultaneously taken from us much of our access to a sense of timelessness. For the symbols of eternity in religious traditions are, by and large, the symbols of awesome power. Existentialism, the characteristic twentieth-century statement of the nature of human existence, bases itself on our radical temporality, seeing human life as condemned to be purely and wholly immersed in time. No escape, it claims, is possible. For Eliade, the evidence of the history of religions indicates that human beings will not long endure such condemnation; they will inevitably seek an experience of escape from time by involving themselves with symbols of the transcendence of time. Nuclear weapons are such a symbol.

The immense power of a nuclear explosion leaves the observer awestruck and therefore unaware of the passage of time. Journalist William Laurence wrote: "On that moment hung eternity. Time stood still."[32] One is transported back to the "big bang," the nuclear explosion with which the universe began: "One felt as though he had been privileged to witness the Birth of the World."[33] At the same time, however, one is also transported forward to the final "big bang," the annihilation that nuclear weapons inevitably symbolize. The Bomb is thus our prime symbol of the alpha and omega of the universe and the whole span of time in between.

The annihilation that we imagine to be brought by the Bomb is an instantaneous one; the button is pushed, the *big whoosh* consumes all, and time ends, just as God intervenes instantaneously at the end of time in Western religious belief. But since the instant of the end is always an imminent possibility, we are in effect living at the time of the end right now. We are, as Jonathan Schell says, now in the process of extinction, or more precisely of self-extinction: "Like death, extinction is felt not when it has arrived but beforehand, as a deep shadow cast back across the whole of life. . . . Extinction saturates our existence and never stops happening."[34]

Yet this very fact creates a new sense of timelessness. A nuclear war would destroy time in any humanly meaningful sense: "The past will not even have been the past—for how would that which merely had been differ from that which had never been? Nor would the future be spared; it would be dead even before being born," writes Gunther Anders.[35] Norman Mailer has suggested that the catastrophes of Hiroshima, Nagasaki, and the concentration camps have already had a similar effect: "Our psyche was subjected to the intolerable anxiety that death being causeless, life was causeless as well, and time deprived of cause and effect had come to a stop."[36] But perhaps this end of history is something we desire, for it means an end to the limits placed on us by our own temporality. To quote Hillman: "We can regard today's concern with mass suicide through the Bomb as an attempt of the collective psyche at renewal by ridding itself of the binds of history and the weight of its material accumulations."[37] If we are already in the process of extinguishing time and history, this may be one more facet of the appeal of the Bomb.

At a time when the end is already symbolically here, where there is no tomorrow, we inevitably live for today: "The hydrogen bomb's power to destroy in an instant all that man has created, and perhaps all that man is, has contributed to one of the general characteristics of our time: a preoccupation with the ephemeral . . . 'The bomb has exploded a lot of myths. Like the myth that there are some things that can't be destroyed. People used to believe that.' "[38] If everything can be destroyed—and, in a sense, is already being destroyed—then there is surely no need to work today for a better tomorrow; in fact, there is no need to worry about tomorrow at all. Thus we face the ethic of living for the moment, which was perhaps most evident in the "now generation" of the 1960s. As George Wald put it, in an often-quoted remark made in 1969:

"What we are up against is a generation that is by no means sure that it has a future."[39]

Members of that generation expressed themselves quite clearly as they reflected on the Bomb: "It kind of makes one accept death as something which will happen, and which should not be taken too seriously. Live life for today and not worry too much about tomorrow. . . . It has put a value on the now, the me, the feelings, not the job, the money, the nice life. . . . Only makes me more convinced of the advisability of living life a moment at a time, irrespective of the last moment or the moment to come, best letting each moment stand full and complete in and of itself."[40] Many aspects of the 1960s counterculture were aimed at transcendence of time through sexual, mystical, and drug experience. It represented a modern-day analogue to the traditional religious desire to escape from the terrors of history.

In the 1980s the young have been characterized as more traditional, more concerned with working today for a better tomorrow. Yet this attitude can coexist with a continuing sense of living only in and for the moment. As an adolescent recently put it: "Everything has to be looked at on two levels,"[41] a level on which there is a future as previous generations knew it, and a level on which there is no future because the end is already upon us. While the first level supports a traditional work ethic, the second can generate what Norman Cousins calls "the disconnected man . . . whose only concern about the world is that it stay in one piece during his own lifetime . . . . Nothing to him is less important than the shape of things to come or the needs of the next generation. Talk of the legacy of the past or of human destiny leaves him cold."[42] In the nuclear age, the young have strong incentives to become the disconnected generation, for there is comfort in the escape from time—and in a continuing connection with the beginning and the end of things through the primary symbol of eternity, the Bomb.

The Bomb is a symbol of eternity on other levels as well. If nothing in this world is permanent, if all things are subject to destruction, perhaps the Bomb itself is the only thing that will endure. If we are all in the front-line trenches of the nuclear confrontation, we may well be persuaded that this situation of confrontation is itself permanent. For in World War I the nature of inconclusive trench warfare led many to the suspicion that peace would never be known again: "One did not have to be a lunatic or a particularly despondent visionary to conceive quite seriously that the war would literally never end and would become the permanent condition of mankind," said Paul Fussell.[43] And perhaps there is a perverse satisfaction in knowing that at least something is stable and can be counted on.

Moreover, the actual use of nuclear weapons in war offers another kind of timelessness; the effects of such a war may well be perceived as being eternal: "Survivors feel themselves involved in an endless chain of potentially lethal impairments, which, if it does not manifest itself in one year—or in one generation—may well make itself felt in the next. . . . [There is] a larger constellation now perceived not as an epidemic-like experience but as a permanent and infinitely transmissable form of impaired mind-body substance" (Lifton).[44] Of course this perception assumes that there will be survivors. As we shall see in later chapters, this assumption is perhaps inevitable, and it is intimately tied to the religious notions of eternity and the return to primal chaos.

Ironically, Jonathan Schell, in his impassioned argument against nuclear weapons, sums up on one page many of the themes that we have tried to relate thus far. A nuclear war, he says, would be

an abyss in which all human purposes would be drowned for all time. . . . The stake is, humanly speaking, infinite. . . . We stand before a mystery. We are in deep ignorance. Our ignorance should dispose us to wonder, our wonder should make us humble, our humility should inspire us to reverence. . . . In trying to describe the possible consequences of a nuclear holocaust, I have mentioned the limitless complexity of its effects on human society and on the biosphere—a complexity that sometimes seems to be as great as that of life itself. But if these effects should lead to human extinction, then all the complexity will give way to the utmost simplicity—the simplicity of nothingness.[45]

The lure of nothingness—the possibility of extinction—has always fascinated human beings and enticed them into situations of lethal risk. There is an intensity about such situations, where we encounter the "bottom line" of life and death, that cannot be matched elsewhere. Even when mortal danger comes unsought, its intensity is memorable. A survivor of Nazi-occupied France said, many years after the war: "My life is so unutterably boring nowadays! Anything is better than to have nothing at all happen day after day. You know that I do not love war or want it to return. But at least it made me feel alive, as I have not felt alive before or since."[46] Similarly, a survivor of a Siberian concentration camp wrote: "In a strange way, despite the horror of it, this also gave a certain richness to our lives. Who knows what happiness is? Perhaps it is better to talk in more concrete terms of the fullness or intensity of existence, and in this sense there may have been something more deeply satisfying in our desperate clinging to life than in what people generally strive for."[47] Thus our embrace of nuclear weapons may reflect the same desire for intensity that is manifest in all warfare, as well as the fascination that the thought of limitless power exerts upon us.

Yet this issue appears more complicated when we observe that, for many, possession of the Bomb does not mean lethal risk but, rather, absolute omnipotence and hence escape from risk. Having an instrument of total destruction at their disposal, governments easily come to believe that they can gain total domination over their enemies. This process may have led United States leaders to use the new bomb against Japan at the end of World War II. Even if it was not a military necessity, it may have been a psychological necessity; one could not have such power at one's disposal and resist the temptation to use it. The same sense of omnipotence may very well extend to all citizens of a country that possesses nuclear weapons. Thus we find support for bigger bombs even when they may be militarily impractical and less useful than small bombs.

This fantasy of total control marks a fundamental difference between religious encounters with limitless power and our modern encounter with the Bomb. Hitherto, those who have placed themselves in relationship with absolute power have accepted a position of dependence, which Rudolf Otto called "creature-feeling." "Creature-feeling" is the radical sense of one's own smallness, or even nonexistence, in the face of infinitely awesome power. Identifying our own personal power with the power of the Bomb, however, we may seek to avoid the risk of nothingness by believing ourselves to have mastered it. In the Bomb's divine omnipotence we find our own omnipotence: "If there is anything that modern man regards as infinite, it is no longer God; nor is it nature, let alone morality or culture; it is his own power. *Creatio ex nihilo*, which was once the mark of omnipotence, has been supplanted by its opposite, *potestas annihilationis* or *reductio ad nihil*; and this power to destroy, to reduce to nothingness, lies in our own hands. . . . It is we who are the infinite," in Anders's words.[48]

So we find ourselves numinous and awe-inspiring, and the ambivalence that we have toward numinous power is directed equally to ourselves. We are afraid of ourselves as bearers of infinitude: "The infinite longing some of us still experience is a nostalgia for finitude, the good old finitude of the past; in other words, some of us long to be rid of our Titanism, and to be men again, men like those of the golden age of yesterday" (Anders).[49] Yet, having a longing for some relationship with infinitude and finding it nowhere else but in our Bomb, we are drawn to the Bomb and the power it offers us as well, and we are loath to give it up. For this infinite power is a magical one—a power that can solve all problems with one quick and sweeping stroke; solving all problems means escaping all limits. Perhaps the ultimate problem, the ultimate limit, is our own paralyzing ambivalence toward ourselves as possessors of the Bomb.

Thus the Bomb offers itself as a solution to the problem it has created. In contemplating the dissolution that attracts us for so many religious reasons, we also contemplate the dissolution of our apparently insoluble dilemma in relating to ourselves. And if this dissolution can come in one swift universal stroke, returning us to a primordial chaos with no strife or tension, what could be more appealing? If there is a single Bomb, of which all nuclear weapons are a part, then there is also a single nuclear holocaust, a single cosmic mushroom cloud, one *big whoosh* in which all reality is returned to its primal state, in which all limits are instantly transcended. Just as God works his will instantly, having no limits upon his power, so does the Bomb, and so do we as masters of the Bomb. In manifesting our infinite power we find the only solution to the problem of our infinite power. Once the button is pushed, there may be no future solutions to our problems, but neither will there be any problems to solve.

2

THE MANY MEANINGS OF "SECURITY"

By starting with the observation that everyone is awed by a nuclear explosion, we have been able to discover a number of similarities between nuclear weapons and religious symbols. However, the importance of religious symbols is not exhausted in exploring this dimension of awesome power. Another equally important side of the religious life, and an equally important symbolic dimension of nuclear weapons, may be revealed if we begin from another observation with which all can agree: nuclear weapons were developed, and continue to be produced and deployed, in the context of a professed concern for national security. Whether this concern is the only or even principal motivation for nuclear armament is surely open to question. But the governments that deploy these weapons, and most of the people ruled by those governments, appear to believe that national security is their overriding concern.

These two observations are not unrelated. The desire for security can easily grow into a desire for invincible omnipotence. The freedom that security is supposed to protect then becomes equated with omnipotence. As we shall see, these developments foster an attitude of extreme dualism; the quest for security turns into a battle of absolute good against absolute evil.

The first atomic bomb was developed, of course, in the context of an all-out drive to defeat an enemy, and especially out of fear that the enemy would develop the Bomb first. While this first enemy soon became an ally, it was supplanted by others, and so the Bomb has continued to be seen as our principal protection from enemy threat. We find ourselves sheltering behind our arsenal of nuclear weapons, as if it were some kind of magical shield out of a medieval legend. It offers an imagined sense of invulnerability, in which Americans may be particularly prone to believe. Because we expect to find absolute protection and absolute safety from a weapon of absolute power, the dualism of "our side" and "the Enemy" becomes absolute too: "Once a nation pledges its safety to an absolute weapon, it becomes emotionally essential to believe in an absolute enemy."[1] The nuclear shield becomes a wall of total separation. Thus Senator Brien McMahon urged the development of the hydrogen bomb not only because it meant "total power" for America, but also because Russia was "total evil."[2]

The nature of modern warfare seems to have been leading in the direction of such absolutism even before the advent of nuclear arms. World War I may have been the first war in modern times marked by a sense of total confrontation between two implacably opposed sides that are radically polarized. Paul Fussell suggests that this new view stemmed from the psychological conditions of trench warfare, which "with its collective isolation, its 'defensiveness,' and its nervous obsession with what 'the other side' is up to, establishes a model of modern political, social, artistic, and psychological polarization."[3] In modern warfare—and certainly in the age of nuclear warfare—the distinction between combatants and noncombatants is virtually erased. In this situation, "whole populations come more and more to be regarded as legitimate objects of annihilation. . . . Restraints on the way the enemy's will to resist is broken down have disappeared. . . . We quickly reach, by benefit of propaganda, that terribly simplified morality with a single absolute: 'Any act that helps my side win the war is right and good, and any act that hinders it is wrong and bad.' This drive toward moral absolutism of a totalitarian sort affects all other aspects of warfare in our age."[4] Hence the enemy as a real flesh-and-blood individual disappears, to be replaced by "the Enemy" as an abstraction that embodies total and unredeemable evil. The only possible attitude toward such evil is to hate it and resolve to use every means to destroy it.

This kind of absolute dualism may be more pervasive in military circles; one Strategic Air Command general opposed a particular policy because "it means less Russians dead. So I'm against it."[5] But in a Cold War in which all citizens are on the front line all the time, such an attitude tends to become universal. And it is both fostered by and reflected in the ideological slogans that serve to legitimate it. These slogans are symbols in themselves (an assertion that need not prejudge their truth or falsity); they join together with the symbolisms of the Bomb to weave a tightly knit fabric of interlocking symbols, which creates an all-enveloping worldview. The key assumptions in this ideological framework are that we stand for freedom and dignity and self-determination, while the other side stands for oppression and degradation and totalitarianism. Yet when it relies on the unlimited power of the Bomb for its preservation, freedom easily comes to mean omnipotence, and oppression comes to mean anything that deprives us of omnipotence. Thus all of the attractions of the omnipotence symbolized by the Bomb are reflected in our ideological commitment to freedom. However, this intimate link of ideology and the Bomb may lead further into absolutism and ultimately to the destruction of the ideology that we hope to protect.

It is impossible to have the freedom of omnipotence when one's perceived enemy has an instrument of absolute power. Yet the "superpowers" seem blind to this obvious fact, and so they pursue the impossible dream of omnipotence simultaneously and, inevitably, endlessly. With both sides already possessing practically unlimited power, neither can ever surpass the other, so each must be forever frustrated and thus forever chasing the other. Yet the impossibility of the goal makes it even more of an absolute goal and leads the "superpowers" to commit themselves ever more absolutely to it.

Not only is our ideological goal one of absolute freedom, but we perceive the Enemy's goal as the absolute cessation of our freedom. Hence we feel compelled to respond with an absolute commitment to destroying the Enemy once and for all; for as long as the Enemy exists, we are by definition less than omnipotent and therefore not really free. Our goal becomes total obliteration of the other, not because of some specific harm the other might inflict upon us, but simply because the other exists. And our possession of weapons of unlimited power makes this goal appear to be attainable, however unrealistic that appearance might be. For if we cannot attain it, how can we ever be truly free?

It might be possible, of course, for two opposing nations, caught in this Catch-22 cycle, to admit their dilemma and work constructively to solve it. "But," writes Lifton, "the more frequent national response resembles that of an individual who fends off his imagery of threatened annihilation by means of more aggressive and more total measures to assert his power, measures which may in turn enable him to believe his illusion of invulnerability. Thus nations, perhaps especially bomb-possessors, are likely to move toward totalism in both foreign and domestic policies."[6] This means that each side, while perhaps believing in its slogans of freedom and self-determination, is inexorably led to attempt to impose itself and its power on the entire world; and governments, in the name of freedom and security, increasingly limit the freedoms of their own people.

A further irony in this attempt to secure ideological victory through the Bomb is, of course, that a nuclear war would destroy the society that seeks to implement its ideology, and thus it would destroy any possibility of realizing the aims for which it was fought. Corpses cannot be free, and there is every likelihood that survivors would live under unprecedented government control and regimentation.[7] But the frustration engendered by the recognition of these ironies does not prevent the pursuit of impossible goals. Rather, the fault is laid on the Enemy; since he is the "aggressor" this intolerable situation must be entirely his doing. It becomes merely one more dimension of his frustration of our omnipotence, and thus the worldview of absolute dualism is further reinforced.

Our frustration is only increased by the insistent feeling that the Bomb ought to offer a simple solution to our insecurities. When it was first developed, the Bomb seemed to be a panacea, an instant solution to all our foreign problems. It was the "hammer,"[8] which could compel anyone to do our bidding. While the development of Soviet nuclear capacity softened this image considerably, it still remains as part of the legacy of thinking in absolutes and as an important aspect of the symbolic meaning of nuclear weapons.

There is something peculiarly satisfying in the image of instantaneous destruction raining down on the Enemy. All we need to do is
push the button, and the magical power will be released in all its
terrifying suddenness—that same magical power inherent in the
thunderbolt of Zeus or the hammer of Thor, which instantaneously
does the bidding of the god who wields it. The inevitable frustration
of our imagined divine powers by an enemy who has equal powers
must make us all the more determined to destroy the enemy.

It is evident, then, that the limitless power embodied in the Bomb
breeds an atmosphere of radical dualism. Such an atmosphere is
nothing new in the history of human culture. Historians of religion
know that every society has been touched by dualism in some
degree; many have been totally immersed in it. In our Western
traditions, security has been seen in a deeply dualistic context, for
security means the maintenance of a divinely created order in the
face of a devil who seeks universal disorder. But the West's dualism
has been tempered by a conviction that the devil is a creature of
God and thus part of God's plan for the cosmos. Monotheism
demands that good and evil must both stem from a single omnipotent source. Indeed, nearly all religious dualisms contain some
symbolic acknowledgment of an infinite reality out of which both
poles have been generated. The ambivalence that religious people
feel toward limitless reality is in part a reflection of that reality's
capacity to embody the extremes of both order and chaos. In the
previous chapter we looked at the lure of disorder and destruction.
Now we must examine the religious meaning of order and the hope
for security in the face of threatening disorder.

This aspect of religion has been elucidated best by sociologists of
religion. They have focused on religious symbols as building blocks
of culture, blocks that create a familiar, stable, comprehensible
human world. From this perspective, religion's principal function is
to create, transmit, and reinforce a coherent worldview and meaning-structure—a nomos—which allows individuals and communities to endure the threat of chaos and meaninglessness.

One of the best-known exponents of this approach is Peter
Berger, who writes that "every socially defined reality remains
threatened by lurking 'irrealities.' Every socially constructed nomos
must face the constant possibility of its collapse into anomy. Seen

in the perspective of society, every nomos is an area of meaning carved out of a vast mass of meaninglessness."[9] To protect itself against the chaos of meaninglessness, the sociologist claims, society sacralizes its nomos: "There occurs a merging of its meanings with what are considered to be the fundamental meanings inherent in the universe. Nomos and cosmos appear to be coextensive."[10] Hence, "To be in a 'right' relationship with the sacred cosmos is to be protected against the nightmare threats of chaos. To fall out of such a 'right' relationship is to be abandoned on the edge of the abyss of meaninglessness."[11]

The Enemy, then, may represent a threat to "our side" on a number of levels. It may threaten our food supply, or our power over other peoples, or the continuity of our particular cultural forms, or any one of a vast number of concrete concerns. And there is little doubt that in the Cold War each side does fear what the Enemy might do to it in such concrete terms. But fundamentally the fear of the Enemy is always fear for "our world"—its order, its stability, and, consequently, its meaningfulness. In a comprehensive survey of perceptions of war in the major religious traditions, James Aho has compiled a large amount of data to support such a conclusion: "The ultimate and universal meaning of sacred combat . . . has been to sustain social order and sanity, to preserve nomos in the face of anomos. . . . In the sacrifice of the warrior, the reality of society is symbolically cleansed of any taint of chaos, and its members are persuaded of its immortality."[12]

This goal of "the protection of the world from nothingness" may be sought in one of two ways. In the "cosmological" approach to war, soldiers fight according to a rigid and ritualized set of rules; their structured activity is in itself a reenactment and therefore a reestablishment of the cosmic order that has been threatened. It is interesting to note that the "cosmological" warrior has many of the traits of the nuclear-age "cold warrior": he wins his victories by means of a magical weapon; he thereby takes on some aspects of the evil he fights against; he must suffer injury in wielding this weapon; this injury, however, guarantees him participation in divine power; he is both fascinating and terrifying, and in general shares in the "coincidence of opposites" in a variety of ways; he gains salvation from his victory. In all of this, however, the goal is not extrinsic to war. Rather, the combat, carried out in accord with the accepted societal structure, is an end in itself.

Aho calls the alternative attitude toward war the "historical" approach. Here there is no blending of opposites, of good and evil. Rather, there is an assumption that every action in history must be either in obedience to or in rebellion against the historico-political order established by a just God. Rebellion is injustice, and it must be opposed by humans as strenuously and absolutely as it is opposed by God. Here, too, we find traits of the "cold warrior": There is absolute dualism; the war is fought for the extrinsic aim of preserving ideological values; war is a "total" phenomenon and any means are justified in pursuit of a just end; the rupture in the world-order is a political rupture, rather than a mythic or natural-cosmic one, and it must therefore be repaired in the political, and military, realm. But again the overriding theme is the maintenance of meaningful order in the face of threatening chaos.

There is little to suggest that this fundamental meaning of war has changed in the modern era. Both world wars were fought by the Allies to defend "our civilization," "our way of life," against an enemy depicted as uncivilized, barbaric, even animal. The land of the Enemy is the land of nothingness; a World War I veteran writes: "In fifty years I have never been able to rid myself of the obsession with No Man's Land and the unknown world beyond it. This side of our wire everything is familiar and every man a friend; over there, beyond their wire, is the unknown, the uncanny."[13] Fussell sums up a phenomenon he finds pervasive in World War I (which was probably equally so in World War II): "The presence of the enemy off on the borders of awareness feeds anxiety in the manner of the dropping-off places of medieval maps [i.e., the edge of the world]. . . . 'Now you know that certain roads lead, as it were, up to an abyss.' " The Enemy's land is that abyss, "the 'other' mysterious, vacant yet impenetrable land."[14]

The advent of nuclear weapons, with their unlimited power, merely heightened this perception of war as the preservation of order and meaning. For once again, as in the past of traditional religions, worldview and meaning-structure are sacralized by being grounded in the sacrality of ultimate power; it is no longer God but the Bomb that guarantees eternal order, but the principle is the same. Thus it is not surprising that a high naval official told sailors manning nuclear weapons that in the event of a nuclear war "you will contribute to the salvation of civilization, for you man the most powerful weapons system ever devised."[15]

It would seem, then, that the concept of "national security," when viewed from the perspective of comparative religion and the sociology of religion, takes on a much broader meaning. Nuclear weapons appear to be prized not only because they are believed to protect one's material goods and ideological values, but more importantly because they are believed to protect one's nomos—the structure of reality itself. Of course the weapons, the material goods, and the ideological values are all parts of the nomos; the nomos might best be seen as the framework of connections that links these and other aspects of our worldview into a (relatively) integrated whole. But the point is that the whole is more valued than any of its parts, and perhaps even more valued than the sum of its parts. Hence even if one part of the nomos is a desire for life, safety, and peace, that part might be sacrificed in order to preserve the whole. And it appears that the fundamental principle governing the whole is absolute dualism—a dualism symbolized by, magnified by, and in part created by the Bomb.

Because it is clear that the Bomb is a key element in our nomos, it becomes equally clear that to renounce dualism and the Bomb voluntarily we must also renounce our very sense of the meaningful order of reality, a renunciation that no one is likely to make voluntarily. In this light, the ineffectiveness of the nuclear-disarmament movement becomes more understandable. Pointing out inner contradictions in the nomos, pointing out that it might lead to its own destruction and the destruction of those human beings who live within it is not likely to be a very persuasive argument. Death itself may be acceptable—even welcomed—if it is made comprehensible and meaningful within the socially sanctioned nomos. As long as the religious person can be in touch with sacred power, and as long as that power serves to give sense and meaning to reality, neither logical contradiction nor suffering nor threat of death are able to undermine the nomos. Conversely, even the lure of logical consistency and perfect safety cannot compensate for the loss of the cherished worldview and meaning-structure.

Thus from the 1950s on we have seen articulate and persuasive arguments illuminating the folly and illusion of pursuing security through the Bomb, the self-destructive and self-defeating nature of an absolutely dualistic worldview imposed on the political process. Yet these arguments fall largely on deaf ears, because behind the deafness is the unspoken question: What is the alternative? And when an alternative is proposed, it inevitably speaks in terms of "universal brotherhood" or "world government" or the like, and it is immediately labeled as unrealistic. In other words, it falls so far outside the socially sanctioned worldview that it seems, quite literally, "not real," and hence it can be seen only as an equivalent to chaos and madness. There is actually more "security," in the broadest and most fundamental meaning of the word, in the familiar and socially acceptable nomos, regardless of its dangers, because it continues to make life meaningful. And it must be admitted that the pieces of the nomos—its material culture, its ideological values, its political perceptions, its absolute dualism, and the Bomb as the symbol of power at its center—do fit together, as long as they are not questioned with too much logical rigor, and that they build on a foundation of dualism that seems to be innate in the human condition. Worldviews take a very long time to develop and a very long time to disappear. Anyone who would have the present dualistic worldview disappear may be hard pressed to offer a meaningful alternative.

At this point, proponents of nuclear armament might want to raise a fundamental objection. They would agree that nuclear weapons are necessary for our national security, but they might want to argue that the meaning of "security" has been misconstrued here. The very existence of nuclear arsenals, they might say, has broken the traditional equation between security and the ability to defeat an enemy militarily. Douglas MacArthur, commander of the only army ever to use nuclear weapons in war, pointed this out early in the nuclear age. The Bomb, he said, "has destroyed the possibility of war's being a medium for the practical settlement of international differences. . . . If you lose, you are annihilated. If you win, you stand only to lose."[16] A 1984 poll found nine out of ten Americans agreeing that "There can be no winner in an all out nuclear war; both the U.S. and the Soviet Union would be completely destroyed."[17] Under these circumstances, security can mean only the certainty that the Bomb will never be detonated in anger. Yet that certainty, many nuclear proponents insist, is given to us only because we have nuclear weapons. The Bomb protects us from itself.

William Laurence, on seeing an early hydrogen-bomb test, reflected that "this great iridescent cloud and its mushroom top . . . is actually a protective umbrella that will forever shield mankind against the threat of annihilation in any atomic war."[18] In the same vein, Winston Churchill advocated nuclear armament with the reasoning that "safety will be the sturdy child of terror, and survival the twin brother of annihilation."[19] As Jonathan Schell points out, this is a fundamentally religious attitude of trust in a superior power for our safety and well-being: "By growing to actually rely on terror, we do more than tolerate its presence in our world: we place our trust in it. And while this is not quite to 'love the bomb,' as the saying goes, it decidedly is to place our faith in it."[20] Yet the historian of religion might well ask whether there is ever faith in a deity without some measure of love or at least attraction to it.

Even proponents of this belief in the Bomb as the prince of peace may have been troubled from the outset by its potential irrationality. Perhaps this is why they chose to call their belief, with a measure of black humor, Mutually Assured Destruction—MAD. MAD became popular in the early 1960s when the previous strategy of "massive retaliation" began to appear self-defeating. It became evident that nuclear arms created an inherent limit on their own use; the government that relied solely on massive retaliation would be too "muscle-bound" for its own good. The MAD policy seemed to solve this problem, for it claimed that we would produce and deploy nuclear weapons only as a means of protecting ourselves by convincing the Enemy that it would be suicidal to attack us.

As a result of this policy shift, our attention was directed even more firmly to the symbolic rather than empirical meanings of the Bomb. MAD has little to do with the actual capabilities or effects of nuclear weapons. Restraint is supposed to be produced only by what both sides think those capabilities and effects are; it is perception alone that really matters. Hence the preoccupation with a "credible" threat. One must convince the other side of one's power to destroy, but one must equally convince oneself and believe in a weapons system that has never actually been used. Moreover, the MAD approach rests on the assumption that the Enemy will imagine the results of war without actually experiencing the situation. It therefore emphasizes imagination and fantasy. Of course fantasy is at work on our side as well. We fantasize the Enemy's intentions without knowing what those intentions are (or would be without the threat of MAD), and thus we compel the Enemy to respond in terms of our own fantasies. We never have a chance to learn what the Enemy would do in the absence of those fantasies.

Psychologists tell us that preventive strategies such as MAD "provide no way of determining whether the action supposedly being deterred would have occurred in the absence of the deterrent, or if a threat that existed when the deterrent was established has ceased to exist. . . . Even if the threat of nuclear attack were originally non-existent, the dynamics of the deterrence process would generate a belief in its reality, and eventually make the threat real. This irony reflects the operation of a self-fulfilling prophecy."[21] In sum, a Cold War based on the MAD doctrine is a war fought with and because of largely symbolic images and perceptions.

But the symbolic dimensions of MAD run much deeper than these strategic considerations. Its fundamental appeal lies in the mental image it creates—an image of an impregnable wall built of bombs, behind which we can shelter safely forever. Like the walls of ancient cities, which separated the chaos without from the order within, this nuclear wall seems to make our nomos perfect and inviolable. Yet like those city walls, it offers protection less from its empirical qualities than from the sacred and magical power it is believed to possess. As long as the wall remains high and sturdy, we believe, neither side in the global conflict can make a significant move. Nothing can alter this stalemate; change itself seems impossible, and thus the "terror of history" and temporality itself are transcended. There is safety in a static eternity.

The potential breach in this magic wall is apparent as soon as we turn to its irrational premise, the MAD-ness of MAD: nuclear weapons remain unusable only as long as each side convinces the other of its willingness to use them. "If the use of nuclear weapons is renounced, they lose their utility not only as weapons of war but as instruments of peace. If deterrence is to work, an aggressor should not be able to dismiss entirely the possibility of nuclear retaliation."[22] In other words, our security depends on our willingness to live every moment not only as front-line trench soldiers but also as perpetual hostages, as Donald Snow points out: "The dynamic that makes the system stable by removing any incentive for initiating a nuclear war is the so-called hostage effect: the ability in any circumstance to retaliate after any first strike and to do unacceptable damage (that is, to kill a prescribed number of people), such that the effect is to hold civilian populations as figurative hostages."[23] Or perhaps we should say "literal hostages."

Even many advocates of the nuclear-weapons buildup have been disturbed by the irrationality of MAD when they realized that it condemned them to the role of nuclear hostages. So they have conceded that in the long run our own best interests would be served by reducing the world's nuclear arsenals through negotiated arms control. Advocates of nuclear deterrence who also embrace arms control have linked the two in the image of a "dual-track" solution that has won acceptance across a wide spectrum of political opinion. The two tracks are generally believed to run side by side because we must protect ourselves with strong deterrence until arms control is successful. But the dual-track image suggests that the two tracks need not be inversely related; that is, more arms control need not mean less deterrent force. Rather, the symbolic meanings shared by the two indicate that both can be equally appealing and that their appeals can be mutually reinforcing. More of one may mean more of the other, and the dual-track could run on forever.

The obvious link between the two tracks is the claim that weapons buildups provide incentive for the other side to negotiate weapons reductions. The underlying assumption here is that the other side does not really want to negotiate in good faith and will agree to equitable arms reductions only under compulsion. This view has been clearly articulated by Edward L. Rowny, a top arms negotiator in the Reagan administration, who concludes: "Above all, we must talk from a position of strength. It is absolutely vital that we rebuild our defenses, for unfortunately it is strength alone that the Soviets understand and grudgingly respect. . . . We must send a clear signal that we are as strongly prepared to defend our interests as we are determined to reach a common ground of agreement."[24] Here the concept of deterrence is taken one step further. The Bomb can deter not only acts of war but also bellicose attitudes. Virtually every recent development in nuclear weaponry has been heralded with the claim that is needed to deter Soviet intransigence and thus reduce nuclear weapons.

Behind this line of thinking lies the traditional conception of the Enemy as a chaotic force, which must be brought under control if our security is to be guaranteed. Our constantly proclaimed goal in arms negotiations, as in all political arenas, is "stability." If the Soviets must be compelled to accept a stable and equitable agreement, then their natural bent must be toward instability. This perception is reinforced by the pervasive American assumption that only the Soviets might ever initiate nuclear war. The unpredictable threat of the Bomb and the unpredictable threat of the Soviets merge together in a generalized feeling that disorder, the true Enemy, threatens us on every side. Both deterrence and arms control are seen as ways to harness and check this threat. This is the most basic meaning of the dual-track image. The two tracks run parallel and work together because both seem headed toward immutably balanced stability. Arms control, like deterrence, is valued as a way to bring the superpowers together into a mutually immobilizing stalemate, immune to the threat of time and change.

The ideal of static balance embodied in the dual-track approach appeals to us in a variety of ways. It demands no choice between the arms race and arms control; the difference between preparing for war and pursuing peace is blurred almost to the vanishing point. Both tracks suggest that newer and better weapons will make us safer. So we can go on increasing the amount of power at our disposal, keep pushing back the limits and bring greater power into our lives, while reassuring ourselves that power and secure order go hand in hand. At the end of the dual-track lies a vision of infinite power contained within infinite order, a perfect "steady state." Perhaps the closest historical analogy is the eighteenth-century

Deist vision of God as a clockmaker creating a cosmic structure that would maintain its universal but delicate balance to all eternity. As *Time* magazine expressed it: "Like the complex interactions within the atom, the volatile forces at work on the planet earth may be able to maintain their dynamic equilibrium indefinitely."[25]

But *Time* added: "That will unquestionably require ever increasing wisdom and skillful management, as well as luck," recognizing the crucial difference between the eighteenth and twentieth centuries: the equilibrium in which we put our faith is now humanly created. The balance we aim at is to be achieved and maintained through human reason. The dual-track image assumes, above all, that the Bomb can be employed rationally as a shield against its own terrors. We can take infinite power into our hands, it tells us, without violating the laws of logic and common sense. We can appropriate the awesome wisdom as well as the omnipotence that our ancestors reserved for God alone.

The widespread acceptance of the dual-track approach reflects the widespread appeal of a fantasy of humanity assuming divine powers. But this fantasy can appeal so easily because it is clothed in the most righteous of moral justifications. If we can forge a perfectly rational and immutable world equilibrium, it would seem to be a victory both for our national strength and for the whole of humanity. What more could anyone, anywhere in the world, desire? We are apparently just as concerned to bring peace and stability to the Russian people as to our own, though they do not realize it. The technological reason we enshrine in the Bomb is equally valid in every nation, for reason tells us that truth is one and the same for everyone. So the eighteenth-century Enlightenment ideal of universal reason can be pressed into the service of twentieth-century politics. But the image of a single infinite power that can save everyone is still very much alive here. The dual-track image suggests that we can use our weapons for universal salvation only if we are strong and unyielding in the Cold-War struggle—firm in both our deterrence posture and our negotiating stance. It implies that we can, and must, form an immovable center around which the world might revolve. Our nuclear arsenal and our national power are imagined as the single saving power, the sacred center of human life that can bring perfect order and nomos to the entire world. In the nuclear age, it seems, every conception of "security" leads back to a dualistic worldview and the equation "freedom = omnipotence."

The vision of an immutable global order marked "Made in the USA" has been the foundation of our nuclear-weapons policy since the first days of the atomic age. In 1945 Secretary of War Henry Stimson wrote to President Harry Truman: "If the problem of the proper use of this weapon can be solved, we would have the opportunity to bring the world into a pattern in which the peace of the world and of our civilization can be saved."[26] The problem, of course, is inescapable: we want to achieve peace, which means not using the weapon, and simultaneously to impose an American pattern upon the world designed to protect "our civilization," which means being willing to use the weapon. However one tries to solve this problem, it always ends up in some version of the Orwellian dictum, "War is peace." Yet all government leaders since Stimson's time have acted as if the problem could be solved— although none has known quite how. Like Stimson, they have affirmed that the Bomb can save us, in some inscrutable way, from every anomic terror, including its own.

The nation as a whole has generally followed its leaders along the dual-track that leaps, like faith, over the chasm of logical contradiction. The same poll that found nine out of ten Americans believing nuclear war unwinnable also found a majority supporting "new and better nuclear weapons." While eight out of ten agree that "there is nothing on earth that could ever justify the all out use of nuclear weapons," that any use of nuclear weapons inevitably means all-out nuclear war, and that "we cannot be certain that life on earth will continue after a nuclear war," nevertheless over half say, "I'd be willing to risk the destruction of the U.S. rather than be dominated by Russia," and only one-third believe that the United States should aim at a policy of never using nuclear weapons.[27]

Yet these paradoxes may hold the key to the deepest appeal of the dual-track image. By linking war and peace, deterrence and negotiation, and arms increases and arms reduction, it suggests that static rational balance can unify every pair of opposites in an apparently coherent whole. Everything can be affirmed; nothing need be given up. Indeed, the more contradictions the policy must face the stronger is its appeal, for each contradiction is further evidence that human reason can fashion a perfectly balanced, all-encompassing synthesis. This vision of perfection seems to assure us that the real Enemy, unpredictable irrational instability, can be vanquished forever. It offers a uniquely modern conception of universal wholeness, binding infinite power to infinite order in an eternal, humanly constructed unity.

Do we really believe that the dual-track policy can provide security? Or have we embraced it simply to justify, and mask the terror of, our possession of infinite power? No doubt there is some truth in both views. But even those most sincerely convinced of the rationality of the dual-track cannot avoid some uneasiness, however unconscious it may be, over the most fundamental contradiction of all: security always rests on a clear demarcation between order and disorder; yet by making the Bomb the foundation of our national security we have made our prime symbol of disorder our prime symbol of order. So we have pinned our security on the one reality that erases the boundary between order and disorder. In this sense, any nuclear weapons policy designed to enhance our security must generate insecurity. When irrationality itself is labeled the most dreaded enemy, the insecurity and anxiety produced by this irrationality must be denied, ignored, and vigorously repressed. But repressed anxiety inevitably generates even more anxiety.

This psychological spiral of insecurity feeds on itself and feeds into the political spiral of insecurity. When each side seeks security through ever more destructive weapons, insisting on matching the other side, the result must be a spiraling insecurity. This is reinforced by secrecy measures and growing defense budgets that make the average citizen feel even more insecure. Under the MAD doctrine, national leaders must feel as insecure as anyone else. They realize that they are hostages to the Enemy, that leaders on both sides are bound together as mutual hostages, and that all are hostage to the weapons they have deployed. Just as MAD interlocks the people of all countries in the hostage effect, so it interlocks the Bombs of all countries. Pushing the button to release one Bomb releases the power of all; the world's nuclear weapons understandably seem to be a single Bomb hanging over the heads of all of us, no matter how high our positions of power.

Highlighting the insecurity produced by the dual-track policy should not obscure the insecurity fostered by other nuclear-weapons strategies. The difference is principally that the dual-track makes it easier to mask the insecurity, while a more traditional war-fighting approach brings it closer to the surface. In both cases, though, the Bomb that symbolizes security must generate insecurity. Yet this hardly invalidates the claim of the Bomb to provide security. On the contrary, if "security" means living meaningfully within the nomos, then every potential threat to it will be countered by a stronger commitment to and reliance on the nomos. It is a psychological axiom that when anxiety arises from an unfamiliar source, our first line of defense is to make it look familiar so it can be dealt with in familiar ways. The anxiety generated by nuclear weapons may be projected onto the Enemy, or spies, or any other convenient target; and the weapons themselves, following the old habit, become the protection from anxiety. The illogic of this is similar to that of the alcoholic who, frightened by his awareness that his drinking habit is suicidal, finds relief from anxiety in the bottle. "Nuclear armaments have become for nations what alcohol is to the alcoholic."[28]

The development of American nuclear strategy itself illustrates this pattern. When the policy of "massive retaliation" created anxiety, the solution was found in nuclear weaponry itself, deployed on the MAD principle. Yet by the early 1970s policymakers claimed to have seen through the illogic of MAD and, anxious about its limitations, solved their anxiety by the development of a "flexible-response" doctrine, including the option of "first-strike capability." This last policy shift reached its culmination—at least for the present—in the revelation that the United States is now preparing to fight a long-term nuclear war of at least six months' duration.[29]

In retrospect, it is apparent that this decade-long process was a response to the massive Soviet nuclear arms program of the 1960s. As long as the United States had superior nuclear capability, the government was able to repress its anxiety sufficiently to give some real place to MAD in its strategy. Yet as soon as that superiority was even mildly threatened, the insecurity could no longer be repressed, and the traditional concept of security through defeat of the Enemy was reasserted. Once again, the source of anxiety was made to look familiar—by seeing it in the familiar context of an absolutely dualistic worldview—and the problem offered itself as the solution.

Yet there is serious reason to question whether the familiar worldview had ever been eclipsed. Daniel Ellsberg has compiled evidence to show that the American government has always been prepared to use nuclear weapons for the traditional purpose of defeating the Enemy: "Every president from Truman to Reagan, with the possible exception of Ford, has felt compelled to consider or direct serious preparations for possible imminent U.S. initiation of tactical or strategic nuclear warfare, in the midst of an ongoing, intense, non-nuclear crisis or conflict."[30] The key point, for Ellsberg, is that in none of these situations was there direct threat of nuclear attack upon the United States. These were preparations for a "first strike." The American government has thus consistently viewed the Bomb as merely one more weapon in its arsenal—a weapon to be used for traditional military purposes. It has persisted in seeing war, fought with all available weapons, as a means of protecting nomos against chaos. Despite the admonitions of Douglas MacArthur, and many others, that war could no longer achieve meaningful objectives, the government has been unable to assimilate this revolutionary change.

When a form of behavior is repeated largely for the sake of repetition—to provide a sense of fixed regularity and unchangeable pattern in life—and when that behavior provides a recurring relationship with limitless power, it can be called a religious ritual. America's nuclear-weapons strategy is only one example of the religious ritualization of the nuclear age. Indeed, the whole gamut of behaviors and attitudes surrounding the Bomb can be viewed as an immense national religious ritual. All allow us to act out our faith that "our world," with its traditional values, endures unscathed despite nearly half a century of nuclear terror.

In the nuclear ritual, we can see ourselves as heirs of the founding fathers, as ready as they were to defend freedom against the tyrants. Eternal vigilance, we can believe, is still the price of liberty. So we can fancy ourselves, as Americans always have, the knights in shining armor, prepared to do battle with whatever wicked beast looms on the horizon. We can espouse the ideals of peace while flexing our muscles and warning of our brave willingness to fight; on both accounts, we can see America as the savior of the world. As long as we have more and better bombs, we can keep alive the traditional American vision of this land as God's chosen land, destined to remain invulnerable and victorious. In the dual-track image, we can see ourselves fulfilling this destiny in a painless and effortless way—just the kind of salvation that Americans have always favored. And in the arms race, with its dazzling technological advances, we can find the satisfactions of material progress so valued in traditional America. Since we now understand the freedom our ancestors fought for as unfettered human control over the world, we easily combine technology and political domination to produce a vision of American progress triumphant.

Yet if the root of all security is the affirmation of order against chaos, the true purpose of the nuclear ritual may be to keep on repeating the old patterns—to keep on redrawing the line between order and chaos—simply to reassure ourselves that the line still exists. We make this line as tangible and vivid as we can by drawing it across the map of the world and giving it a name: the Iron Curtain. The more the Bomb blurs the difference between order and chaos, the more we need the Iron Curtain to convince ourselves that a meaningful difference still exists. Rather than need the Bomb to protect ourselves against the threat of "the Russians," we may need "the Russians" to protect ourselves against the Bomb's threat of total anomie. So we use the nuclear ritual to act out our affirmation of traditional values and our implacable opposition to the Enemy, and we combine the two in the many meanings of "security."

The nuclear ritual, like all rituals, has its priests—the "experts" whose technical reasoning grasps complexities supposedly beyond the ken of the average person. These experts set an example of dispassionate rationality that reaches to the highest office in the land. According to *Time* magazine: "The horror of nuclear war has greatly troubled every President, and yet all of them since 1945 have conditioned themselves to plan nuclear strategy coolly and prudently. The experts tend to agree that too much fear in the Oval Office would warp judgment and make crises more likely."[31]

Government and media urge the average person to follow this example; antinuclear protesters are often criticized not for their goals but for their passionate fervor and their open admission of fear. Simultaneously, of course, the experts are objects of awe. They seem to hold numinous mysteries in their hands as they claim to control the infinite power of the Bomb. So the nation identifies itself with its leaders and experts, trying to combine logical structure with numinous might.

Ultimately the nation, its leaders, its experts, and its Bomb are all experienced as a single reality. The average person, bringing this overarching reality into ordinary life by identifying with the nation, gains a structure, meaning, and unlimited power unavailable anywhere else. Participating in a power that is felt as divine, the average person can feel divine. But this is a mixed blessing. While it is exhilirating to merge with the God of our ancestors, it is also terrifying. The freedom we hope to enshrine in the Bomb—freedom from human finitude—is potentially the most anomic experience imaginable. So we feel compelled to follow our nuclear priests, who alone seem able to bring infinite power into some static rational structure.

This is the fundamental goal of all religious ritual. It does not intend to remove the awesome and threatening aspects of limitless reality altogether. It merely intends to bring us into continuing contact with that reality in familiar, time-tested, and hence apparently safe patterns. It attempts to meld the structure of "security" and the infinitude of "freedom" by creating a humanly constructed and humanly controlled encounter with infinite power. Therefore it tends to increase the attraction and fascination of the sacred while diminishing the fear. We value ritual not because it removes the terrifying threat of dissolution and annihilation but because it seems to contain that threat and make it endurable. In fact, ritual must retain some measure of the threat, and the anxiety it breeds, if it is to have compelling power. The nuclear ritual is all the more valuable to us because it offers a heightened sense of controlled terror.

The subtle interweaving of order and disorder, comprehended and incomprehensible, controlled and uncontrollable, confronts us at every turn as we explore the world of the Bomb. The more we ritualize nuclear weapons the more we focus on the orderly, and rationalize or ignore the chaotic. Yet the irrationalities of the nuclear age can only be covered over, never swept away. The upshot is a continued and compounded confusion of rationality and mystery, now largely hidden from view and therefore even more disturbing. So the cycle turns again: confusion breeds more threat of instability and disorder; we cling more tenaciously to the familiar structure; we fear the Enemy ever more intensely, prepare for war ever more assiduously, and rely on the Bomb ever more fervently. Alternatives to the nuclear ritual are overlooked or cast aside because they seem more anomic than the Bomb itself. We trust in the rationality of the "experts" to manage and contain the threat. But the result is simply a deeper feeling of insecurity and anomie.

Having set out to examine the orderly and rational side of nuclear weapons, we have nevertheless arrived back at a place of irrational paradox. Yet because we are unaware of our irrational motives we can believe that we are thinking and acting rationally. And there is a logic here. But it is the special logic of religious symbols, which is also the logic of the nuclear age. It is a logic that enfolds both reason and unreason, finding room for every paradox in an overarching unity that is more compelling and fulfilling than any merely rational logic. Understanding this logic of the symbolic level helps us to understand our insistence on keeping and expanding our nuclear arsenals, despite all truly logical arguments to the contrary.

3

FATE AND CHANCE

In exploring the many meanings of "security," we have encountered many paradoxes that are characteristic features of religious experience. In addition to the paradox of rationality and irrationality, for example, we have noticed that the limitless power that apparently gives us omnipotence also deprives us of our sense of control and power. Like all sacred realities, it heightens that "creature-feeling" that always marks encounters with the numinous. These two paradoxes have a special relationship to each other in the nuclear age. When creature-feeling grows out of a sense of the omnipotent order and structure we aim at with our Bomb, it can easily lead to a feeling of total rigidity and unalterable fate. When creature-feeling reflects a sense of the irrational caprice of omnipotent power, on the other hand, it can just as easily lead to a feeling of total randomness and chance. Both of these are common responses to the overwhelming might of the Bomb.

Fatalism about nuclear war seems to ebb and flow in the public mind. It reached a high point during the early 1960s, when as Edwin Shneidman writes, "a kind of fatalistic popular culture had developed about nuclear weapons. Fueled by novels and motion pictures like *On the Beach* and *Dr. Strangelove*, an air of madness and inevitable doom surrounded the entire issue of strategic weapons and doctrine. Prophecies of nuclear Armageddon were commonplace and widely believed."[1] The increased awareness of the nuclear issue in the 1980s may well reflect another high tide of such feeling.

Public-opinion polls show that a majority of Americans believe that their chances of survival, even in a "limited" war, are poor. Yet few work actively to prevent such a war; few even think about it frequently. One recent poll found that, while 89 percent of the populace thinks their chances of survival in a limited war are no better than 50–50, only 19 percent worry frequently about the threat of war.[2] Many of those who do not worry would probably agree with the student who said: "There is no use worrying about something over which one has no control. If it happens, it happens. . . . If destruction comes, I'll accept it. Everyone must die sometime,"[3] and perhaps with the Hiroshima survivors who explained their survival: "In my case I have a good destiny and this is more than just coincidence. I look upon this kind of destiny as something beyond the personal effort we make—perhaps not exactly the influence of God—but something beyond the personal will, which controls human existence. . . . Because of this experience, I have become a fatalist. . . . It was the Goddess of Fortune that saved me."[4]

Fatalism both reflects and fosters a sense of personal helplessness, and this too was voiced by survivors of Hiroshima: "From all around I heard moans and screaming. . . . I thought that I too was going to die in that way. I felt this way at that moment because I was absolutely unable to do anything at all by my own power."[5] This feeling of utter inability to help oneself persisted long after the immediate effects of the A-bomb attack, so that the Japanese "have used 'A-bomb beggars' to describe the kind of *hibakusha* who has surrendered all autonomy in favor of a continuous plea for help. . . . Prior conflicts over dependency are magnified to the point of dominating one's existence."[6] While not all *hibakusha* have remained quite so helpless, many do feel a sense of resignation in the face of life's events.

Such an attitude may be life-enhancing for those compelled to endure a great disaster. For those who have not actually experienced nuclear war, but live in a country actively preparing for it, a sense of helplessness may be much less positive yet equally pervasive. The Americans interviewed by psychologist Michael Carey pictured themselves as totally helpless victims in a nuclear war, doomed to suffer from the Bomb's all-pervading omnipotence. The

same feeling of total impotence surrounds attitudes toward the
Bomb awaiting use.[7] The average person is likely to leave decisions
on the nuclear issue to the government: "The awesome power of
the bomb is held by the elite; I am not the elite, so I can't influence
the possibility of destruction. That bothers me, but only when I
think about it."[8] Increasingly, those who express support for the
use of nuclear arms in a given situation say "they should use them"
rather than "we should use them." Apparently Americans increasingly divorce the government, which wields the weapons, from
themselves.

But it is questionable whether the elite and the government feel
any more control than the average citizen. Albert Einstein, on
hearing that the hydrogen bomb would be produced, responded
that "the ghostlike character of this development lies in its apparently compulsory trend. Every step appears as the unavoidable
consequence of the preceding one. In the end, there beckons more
and more clearly general annihilation."[9] During the Cuban missile
crisis, the closest the world has yet come to nuclear war between
the superpowers, "President Kennedy had initiated the course of
events, but he no longer had control over them,"[10] according to the
memoirs of Robert Kennedy. An analysis of the events of that
period bears out this judgment; too many factors were beyond the
President's control, and "the efforts to bring American policy under
central direction must be said to have failed."[11] Two decades later,
the President, who supposedly had the Bomb at his disposal, was
still at the disposal of the Bomb. This is reflected in the language of
nuclear war strategists: "The weapons are pictured as having their
own quarrel to settle, irrespective of human purposes."[12] The
interlocking system of nuclear arms around the world, all joined by
commitments to mutual retaliation, creates a community of weapons that has a life of its own beyond human control.

Psychologists suggest that this feeling of impotence on the part of
leaders may reflect a real inability to act constructively to change
the situation. In part this comes from terror at the sheer power of
nuclear weapons. The greater our fear, the less our ability to
respond in creative ways or search for new adaptive solutions to
problems. So those who possess weapons of omnipotence are most
likely to want to use them in traditional military ways. Thus

political leaders capitulate, as it were, to the weapons and the inevitability of their use. It has also been argued that this inability to act reflects a sort of mass state of depression, which arises, according to one analysis, because in the nuclear age one cannot destroy one's enemy without destroying oneself as well. Therefore one cannot express aggression toward one's enemy without simultaneously expressing it toward oneself, creating the state of inner-directed aggression that is the essence of depression. Psychologically, then, as well as politically and militarily, the Bomb seems to turn its masters into servants. But the situation may be even more complex.

The feeling of powerlessness and victimization, although intensified by nuclear weapons, was a dominant feature of the modern age before these weapons were invented. Mass culture, mass technology, and mass political movements—some leading to totalitarianism—all created an increasing sense that individuals counted for little and could do little to shape the circumstances of their lives. Historians tell us that a similar situation arose in the Hellenistic world created by the conquests of Alexander the Great. But the response then was not for individuals to try to reassert control of their own lives; much more common was the decision to make the goddess Fate, or some equivalent, an object of religious worship. Thus it may not be surprising that Norman Cousins describes the proponent of nuclear armament as "a man who not only believes in his own helplessness but actually worships it. His main article of faith is that there are mammoth forces at work which the individual cannot possibly comprehend, much less alter or direct. And so he expends vast energies in attempting to convince other people that there is nothing they can do."[13] Here nuclear weapons both epitomize the problem—twentieth-century mass society; and come to symbolize the solution—the worship of human impotence. Perhaps this is the proper context in which to understand the "missile gap," that pervasive and avidly accepted belief that "we are falling behind the Enemy" in accumulating weapons. While such a view is in part manipulated by special interests who wish higher budgets for the military, it is in part a reflection of the desire to believe in one's own powerlessness.

Why, then, do people seek out and embrace the feeling of

inevitability and helplessness summed up in the worship of Fate? To some extent it is a means of avoiding personal responsibility. This is apparent in the willingness to believe that the government is and must be totally in charge, an attitude that the government no doubt encourages. There may also be a wishful sense of optimism at work here, a belief that progress is inevitable (particularly characteristic of Americans) and that therefore in time the problem will somehow work itself out, without any help from us. Moreover, the sheer immensity of the nuclear-weapons problem staggers us when we try to form some personal engagement with it: "What stuns or panics us at some moments," writes Gunther Anders, "is the realization not of the danger threatening us, but of the futility of our attempts to produce an adequate response to it. Having experienced this failure we usually relax and return shamefaced, irritated, or perhaps even relieved, to the human dimensions of our psychic life commensurable with our everyday surroundings."[14] Psychologically, then, we may feel more at ease with ourselves when we perceive ourselves as helpless.

But fatalism is a religious as well as a psychological phenomenon; only by understanding its religious dimension can its appeal be fully understood. Fatalism, with its insistence on human impotence, consists of a heightening of the "creature-feeling" of which Rudolf Otto spoke. But this feeling arises only when one feels oneself in relationship with numinous power. And relationship means some sort of participation. Thus worship of the goddess Fate is essentially a way to participate in the power that controls all and hence a way to give meaning to life. Today it is the Bomb which controls all, which can reshape or even end all of history. Although I as an individual may be without power, I as a creature in submission to the Bomb am imbued with its power. But I can share in this power only if I first believe in my own powerlessness. Moreover, the effects of the Bomb's power are global in scale; the fate that is in store for me also awaits all humanity. Therefore, in submitting myself to it, I am escaping from the narrow confines of my petty life into something universal and cosmic in import. And this power contains a magical secret, "the secret of the universe." Participation in it allows me to transcend the limits of my ignorance, if only vicariously, and share in the potency of secret wisdom. Thus many may be led to rely on the government and its "experts" because only they are truly privy to the secret; helplessness here fosters the religious value of fatalism. In sum, fatalism can make us feel important, powerful, perhaps even extraordinary, junior partners with the power that can bring the apocalypse.

For many people, the inevitability of Fate also implies a preexisting plan for history. In the Western religious traditions, this view is particularly congenial, for the events of history are held to be manifestations of the omnipotent God. And for the soldier it may be especially attractive too, as Glenn Gray remarks: "The professional soldier feels the need to reduce the capriciousness of his world as much as possible. He chooses to conceive an orderly universe with stable and traditional values, in which death must have its rank and time like everything else. . . . He concludes that there is nothing haphazard about the progress of events, whatever the outward appearance may be."[15] In a global trench-war which puts us all on the front line, it may be that all of us are attracted to this soldier's view of things. The fatalism surrounding the Bomb thus speaks to us of a dependable, structured world and makes us an integral part of that enduring order, as well as putting us in direct (albeit subordinate) relation with the power at the center of the order.

In the Hellenistic world, many people found consolation in the maxim that "Fate leads the willing and drags those who resist." Thus it was obviously advisable to consent to and even affirm one's fate, whether it be fortune or poverty, joy or pain, life or death. The attitude derived from this worldview was Stoicism, the calm and self-possessed embrace of Fate. The pursuit of life and pleasure was rejected, as was the avoidance of death and pain; only an impassive acceptance of one's inevitable role in the cosmic scheme of things was valued. Perhaps the widespread fatalism in the face of the nuclear threat today is analogous to this aspect of Stoicism.

Yet the frantic pursuit of pleasure on the part of many contemporary fatalists belies this analogy. Part of the Stoic vision is followed—that part which sees working for future advantage as foolish. There is in fatalism and powerlessness a strong support for the "live for the moment" ethic that provides a sense of the "eternal Now," the transcendence of time. But the Stoic would not have sought refuge from enemies behind a barricade of bombs, the way the modern nuclear fatalist does. Thus the Bomb again appears to symbolize ambivalent messages: its proliferation is endurable because fatalism makes pain and death meaningful (as part of the necessary cosmic scheme) and therefore endurable. But its proliferation is also endurable, and even desirable, because it is seen as the symbol of protection from pain and death.

It may be argued that fatalism is both a result and a further spur to pessimism about life, and there is surely some truth in this. Pessimism can easily produce the thought that the inevitable destruction might be a good thing, particularly if it means the chance to start over again, and this thought weakens the will to resist fate. But optimism and pessimism are ambiguous concepts in the nuclear age. While optimism is in one sense a preventive to war, we have noted above that optimistic belief in progress can lead to complacency. And while it seems obvious that fatalism is a pessimistic view, it now appears that there is a good deal of optimism in it as well, for it provides the opportunity to transcend our isolation, our insignificance, and our sense of victimization on condition that we embrace our Fate and follow it willingly. To embrace our Fate means, for many, to embrace the nuclear weapons that symbolize that Fate.

In the nuclear age, as in the Hellenistic age, the pervasive feeling of powerlessness need not necessarily lead to a worship of Fate. It may just as easily result in the worship of another equally alluring goddess—Chance. Chance is, to use a key word of this "postmodern" age, absurdity. When all of us, even the President, have come under the power of the Bomb, there is clearly a large element of uncertainty at the center of our lives. If the Bomb has a wisdom of its own, then this uncertainty may only reflect our limited capacity to understand. But if the Bomb is seen as itself an irrational or capricious thing, then the uncertainty is inherent in the nature of things, and reality itself is subject to the absurdity of Chance.

Moreover, the complexities of nuclear strategy seem to dictate that an element of chance must be present if the MAD policy is to save us from war. "It was found that uncertainty is a part of all deterrence. It is by no means certain that a government would wage a suicidal war, destroying an enemy in the process, rather than surrender unconditionally. Nevertheless, it is possible, and it would be unwise to force such an extreme choice."[16] This element of chance was most prominent in the "brinksmanship" of the 1950s: "The brink is a curved slope that one can stand on with some risk of slipping."[17] "It is the deliberate creation of a recognizable risk of war, a risk that does not imply complete control."[18] But it remains an element in all nuclear strategy to the present day. In order to keep the other side guessing, one must introduce a certain amount of unpredictability into the system and thus become the victim of the randomness that one has created.

There is an equal element of uncertainty in the effects of nuclear war. This was true for the very first nuclear explosions, whose effects were much greater than predicted. It remains true for any given explosion and especially for the cumulative effects of many simultaneous explosions, since no one has ever actually experienced the synergistic multiblast situation that would occur in a nuclear war. Paradoxically, though, government planning for war rests on the assumption that such planning can be done rationally and that our leaders are sane, reasonable men who will implement these plans rationally. Even MAD-ness is held to be perfectly rational. When the most sophisticated techniques of logical analysis and prediction are pressed into the service of this realm of illogic, the triumph of randomness and Chance seems to be complete.

Yet Chance, like Fate, has triumphed before in the religious life of humanity, receiving worship as a goddess both formally, during the Hellenistic age, and informally, during the modern era. Ever since Feodor Dostoevski, the gambler, the apostle of Chance, has been an understandable and often admired culture hero, who stands against the total domination of the all-encompassing "system"—the societal structure with no meaning or purpose other than its own pointless self-perpetuation. The gambler refuses to be merely a piano key playing a fated note; he would rather take his chances—take his Chance—and take solace in knowing that there is still a place for unpredictability and caprice. Whether that caprice is self-willed or, as with the gambler, beyond one's control, seems to be a secondary question. The essence is the satisfaction of knowing that there is unpredictability. And so the randomness inherent in nuclear weapons, the irrationality that inevitably accompanies them, generates that same ambivalence of fear and fascination which surrounds the gambler. There is an excitement, an intensity, around the gambling table that can hardly be matched anywhere else in human life. The higher the stakes, the greater the excitement.

Thus the Bomb becomes the symbol for the ultimate gamble, the cosmic crap game. This appears clearly in the horrifyingly naïve words of the high school student who said: "At any second the world might blow up in my face. It makes living more interesting."[19] And it must be admitted that rebellion against the overwhelming "system" is in large part rebellion against the boredom that comes from total predictability. Boredom is intensified, of course, by the psychic numbing that makes the traditional excitements of human life ineffectual for the modern person. Even constant talk of nuclear war becomes boring, so that, as E. P. Thompson points out, after a while only action can be truly exciting. He suggests that this is the main motive behind the renewed talk of "winning" a nuclear war; only if there are winners and losers can the excitement of gambling exist.[20] In the modern quest for new thrills, new kicks, new intensities of sensation, all paths may have to lead to the Bomb. For what one is seeking is actually power, and any given quantity of power becomes boring once one is exposed to it for long enough. But unlimited power combined with randomness is the ultimate thrill, and perhaps the only one with which the modern world can be satisfied.

At the same time, however, there is an uneasiness, even a fear, surrounding the embrace of Chance. Like Einstein, many of us are hesitant to believe that God plays dice with the universe. In the event of a nuclear war, could our chances of survival have nothing to do with justice or our personal worthiness? Those who survived the Hiroshima bombing were apparently deeply troubled by this issue: "The survivor's concern about 'accidents of survival' reflect his profound feeling that he was 'saved' by an unknowable destiny or fate which he must both constantly propitiate and view with uneasiness—since these same larger forces willed the death of so many others. Survivors feel that they 'owe a death' not only to God or Destiny, but to the actual A-bomb dead."[21] Whether one's God be Fate or Chance, survival means deep guilt feelings toward the dead and a dreadful fascination toward the divinity that left one alive. Today, when the Bomb as a potential instrument of future war is itself the embodiment of the force of Fate or Chance, the guilt may well be toward the future victims of nuclear war, victims of the helplessness that we willingly accept and worship—but the dread and fascination remain the same.

4

UNREALITY AND MADNESS

The aura of randomness surrounding the Bomb is just one piece of a larger constellation of themes that inevitably arise from any experience of limitless reality. Infinitude, and the symbols in which it is expressed, must evoke a sense of incomprehensible paradox, ineffability, and hence irrationality. These themes may be more or less prominent in different religious traditions, but they are always present, along with concomitant feelings of the uncanniness and "total otherness" of the sacred. In every religious experience, then, there is some degree of the alien—of departure from normal human reality and reason—and hence some touch of madness. As we encounter nuclear omnipotence, these features take on a special shape and a special prominence, which we shall now explore.

Nearly everyone has been touched by the feeling that the Bomb and its threat are not real: "I've always felt the bomb to be an ineffable thing. . . . Every now and then I have a fantasy that it isn't real at all, that it doesn't exist. . . . It has to do with a sort of magic as well. . . . It undercuts the sense of reality."[1] Faced with such feelings, we, like the *hibakusha* of Hiroshima, may sense that all attempts to talk about the ineffable are doomed to failure. Nevertheless, we do feel the need for words, but inevitably we are led to speak and think in familiar terms. Although words such as *defense, security,* and even *war* may not be relevant to the actuality of the nuclear age, they are the only vocabulary we know. They appeal to us because they reinforce our psychological tendency to deny change (and the possibility of change); they offer us at least the appearance of reassurance. The same phenomenon was evident in World War I, where some suggested that the new reality beggared description; there were no words in the old language, it was claimed, to fit this new reality.

Yet, as Fussell says, "Logically there is no reason why the English language could not perfectly well render the actuality of trench warfare: it is rich in terms like blood, terror, agony, madness."[2] But the capacity of language to fit reality was denied because it was comfortable to deny it: "Soldiers have discovered that no one is very interested in the bad news they have to report."[3] The same may very well be said of those who try to describe in advance the reality of nuclear war. One must make an effort to shape and assimilate the new language, and very few seem inclined to do so. When a few gifted artists find the language, there is a very limited audience to receive it, as Alvarez notes: "The real resistance now is to an art which forces its audience to recognize and accept imaginatively, in their nerve-ends, not the facts of life but the facts of death and violence: absurd, random, gratuitous, unjustified, and inescapably part of the society we have created."[4]

Even if we want to face the new reality brought about by the Bomb, however, our lack of experience with anything even remotely comparable makes it difficult to do so. Lifton found that the *hibakusha* of Hiroshima understood this well: "The apocalyptic nature of the experience, along with the taint of its resulting identity, create a semi-mystical quality which the uninitiated cannot be expected to grasp. Hence I encountered such comments as: 'We have a different feeling from other people who have not experienced the A-bomb'; 'If you haven't seen it with your own eyes, you can't understand it.' "[5]

This atmosphere of ineffability is reinforced by our inability to conceive of our own death as a reality: "The extensive emphasis upon ever more powerful nuclear armaments in the effort to become more 'strong and secure,' despite the deadly risk that is involved, suggests that many people are motivated more by fears of weakness and helplessness than by fears of death. . . . The fact that people have not had the subjective experience of death, as well as the widespread unconscious illusion of one's own invulnerability, may contribute to the lesser psychological 'reality' of annihilation, as compared to that of being defeated and forced to submit" (Group for the Advancement of Psychiatry).[6] Thus the slogan "Better dead than red" and other such affirmations of our ideologies are powerful enough to mask the reality of nuclear war from us.

Similarly, we are unable to conceive of a "dead world," a world in which no humans survive, and therefore we cannot confront a war that would destroy humanity as a real event. As Fornari expresses it:

> Since in our minds the idea of the destruction of humanity "to the last man" as a possible event coincides with the idea of suppression of man as a subject capable of witnessing and verifying the destruction, the very fact of thinking of the extermination of man coincides with the impossibility of regarding it as a really verifiable event. In this connection I was told by someone that the idea of a possible nuclear catastrophe where there would be no survivors did not upset him but that the thought of even one man surviving the catastrophe filled him with anxiety.[7]

This is not a question of the cliché "survivors envying the dead." It is, rather, that if the man pictured nuclear war as having even one survivor, he could then project himself into the role of that survivor and consequently be forced to face nuclear war and his own death in it as a real possibility. But if there were to be no survivors then there is no perspective from which the imagination could deal with the possibility at all. "A person might reason that even if mankind did perish he wouldn't have to know anything about it, since in that event he himself would perish. There might actually be something consoling in the idea of having so much company in death."[8]

As soon as we make any attempt to think about a nuclear war as a real event, however, we must posit a survivor through whose eyes we see the event. Doing so, we may be falsifying reality. But we are offering ourselves the consolation that, despite all the destruction, humanity will survive. From this assumption it is but a short step to the further consolation that "our world," "life as we know it" will survive, and another short step to the asumption that some of our basic values and social institutions—those very things for which we would fight—will survive. Hence nuclear war comes to appear justifiable, or at least a grim necessity. Our own suffering and death, and (perhaps more easily) the suffering and death of others, take on meaning as we posit this basic continuity of our ideological values.

One psychiatrist has looked closely at this issue, however, and found it the crux of the true "madness" of nuclear weapons: "The fact that one's ideological love object is imagined as existing, even though the whole world may be destroyed, seems comprehensible only on the basis of the intervention of a strong mechanism of denial of destruction and loss . . . whereby—in extreme cases— existence is confused with non-existence, and the most forceful affirmation coincides with the most forceful denial."[9] This interpretation leads to the conclusion that we can experience the effects of nuclear war only in terms of the illusory fantasies of the unconscious, in which the love object can be destroyed and preserved simultaneously. "Thus we find ourselves confronted with an unforeseen situation leading to the following hypothesis: In order to be able to perceive the catastrophic situation as a real historical situation, each of us must somehow associate himself with an illusory catastrophic situation relating to our sadistic attacks against our love object."[10] Such sadistic attacks occur (for the vast majority of us) only in fantasy; yet such fantasies do generate guilt, which may become the source of pathological or even psychotic processes. "It would appear to follow that the possibility of facing realistically the problems of the catastrophic age involves treating as an instrument of verifying reality something which we are accustomed to consider a psychotic process. What we are accustomed to call madness may, then, become an instrument of verifying reality."[11]

Madness and fear of madness are intimately linked with the sense of unreality and absurdity symbolized by the Bomb. Something as simple as an airplane or a fire siren can raise a whole cluster of issues concerning reality and sanity in a terrifying, gut-level way. Carey writes that "A poet from Philadelphia still wonders if the loud sirens he hears as a normal part of urban life might be a warning that nuclear war is imminent. How can he tell if this is 'It'? How can he suggest to others that nuclear war might be underway without raising doubts about his sanity?"[12] And the doubts will come not only from the others, but also from himself, as he is forced to find both total normalcy and totally horrifying abnormality signaled by the same siren. How can he have any sane standard to distinguish between them?

Those who have actually experienced the Bomb were also touched by the feeling of craziness in a special way; Lifton suggests that they experienced a "lived-out psychosis" in experiencing "death in life," and he asks "whether or not it created an inner 'knowledge' of the psychotic state—or even a tendency to resort to psychotic-like behavior under certain forms of stress—without lapsing into full-blown psychosis. When *hibakusha* did describe others' 'going crazy' at the time of the holocaust, their details were often vague and the image seemed to be another manifestation of the aura of absolute power surrounding the weapon—of the feeling that anyone exposed to it should have gone crazy."[13]

Craziness is, of course, a very unpleasant feeling, and we will go to great psychological lengths to avoid it. Thus the survivors of Hiroshima overwhelmingly shut themselves off emotionally not only from the event that haunted them but also, by necessary extension, from large parts of life itself: "The survivor undergoes a radical but temporary diminution of his sense of actuality in order to avoid losing this sense completely and permanently; he undergoes a reversible form of symbolic death in order to avoid a permanent physical or psychic death."[14] This is the process that Lifton calls "psychic numbing." And many have agreed with Lifton that the same process characterizes those facing the possibility of future nuclear annihilation, that is, all of us.

But psychic numbing is not simply a product of denial. As Lifton sees it, its roots are more complex, and a fuller understanding of it leads to the conclusion that even those who resolve to confront the true reality of the Bomb are inevitably caught in the web of craziness. Psychic numbing is a result of the loss of an essential component of human life: images and symbols of life-continuity which make the death of the individual endurable. These symbolic modes of "immortality" may be in terms of one's offspring, one's lifework, one's personal survival in religious terms, or merely the survival of the world itself; but all give the individual the capacity to confront, in however limited a way, the reality of death. In our century, however, death has come increasingly to appear as total annihilation—the ultimate cessation of life not only for the individual but for the whole world. And the Bomb has been the chief cause as well as the chief symbol of this new perception of death.

It would seem that the more one pursues a realistic confrontation with the effects of nuclear weapons, the more one is immersed in this vision of utter annihilation—the more one fuses every image of death with the total extinction of the Bomb. Yet the burden of the absurdity of "total death" is too great for most of us to bear; thus the result is a sort of "double life" in which we must deny the reality that we nevertheless know is true. Although we cannot escape the craziness of living constantly under the shadow of annihilation, we usually manage to repress it. We go about our "business as usual," acting as if the danger did not exist, and thus deadening our sensitivity precisely where we need it most. The threat of nothingness paralyzes us and forces us to lose touch with reality: "If extinction is nothing, we may unconsciously ask ourselves, may not no reaction be the right one?" asks Schell.[15]

The madness that pervades our reality is further fostered by the role of government. In the psychiatrically oriented view, the Bomb is necessarily a reflection of our individual unconscious wishes as well as fears; yet it is produced and maintained by the state. Thus the state acquires a monopoly on our fantasies of total destruction. This alienates individuals from their own unconscious lives, and therefore, Fornari says, "faced with the prospect of the destruction of mankind, we feel neither violent nor guilty, as though we are all involved in a gigantic delusion of negation of the external as well as of our internal reality."[16] Thus our reality-testing is further impaired, and a sort of craziness is even more inevitable.

One need not follow the intricacies of such theorizing, however, to appreciate the government's role in fostering our sense of unreality. One need only see that the government takes the leading role in treating nuclear weapons as merely one more instrument of state policy, merely one more military device; in other words, the government more than the population at large acts as if there has been only quantitative, not qualitative, change since 1945. This may be a reflection of the government officials' particular bind: they are apparently in control of the greatest technological power ever created, and yet they know that they are powerless to control world events, or even events in their own nation, and they sense that they are in the Bomb's power, rather than vice versa. Thus they are impelled to deny the reality with which they must deal, and they continue to act as if nothing had changed, as if they still had the power to shape and determine events.

Of course elected officials do admit that the complexity of the world they face is greater than ever before, and thus they willingly, sometimes eagerly, rely on "experts." In the field of nuclear weapons, these experts are known as "strategic theorists" or "defense-intellectuals"; they have perhaps done the most to create the air of unreality surrounding the whole issue. For these theorists have insisted that nuclear war must be amenable to rational analysis and planning. The most famous of these intellectuals, Herman Kahn, writes: "Some feel that we should consider these problems but view them with such awe and horror that we should not discuss them in normal, neutral, professional everyday language. I tend to disagree, at least so far as technical discussions and research are concerned. One does not do research in a cathedral. Awe is fine for those who come to worship or admire, but for those who come to analyze, to tamper, to change, to criticize, a factual and dispassionate, and sometimes even colorful, approach is to be preferred."[17]

Thus it becomes possible to speak of "mega-deaths," of "acceptable kill ratios," of "countervalue attacks" (i.e., the instantaneous obliteration of huge cities); to reduce it all to mathematical models and computer projections; to discuss the death of hundreds of millions of human beings on one day; and all of this in the dispassionate and even colorful language of technical expertise. These technicians have been vigorously criticized for their apparent lack of feeling, and even Kahn hints that there might be a problem here: "It does indeed take an iron will or an unpleasant degree of detachment to go about this task. Ideally it should be possible for the analyst to have a disciplined empathy. In fact, the mind recoils from simultaneously probing deeply and creatively into these problems and being conscious at all times of the human tragedy involved."[18] And so the strategic theorists choose "probing deeply" and shut out the human tragedy. The three-dimensional reality of human life is reduced to the flatness of charts, graphs, and computer bytes. To compound the problem, "The strategist must incessantly plan for future attacks and counterattacks whose prevention is supposedly the planning's whole purpose. Strategic thinking thus refers to a reality that is supposed to never come into existence."[19]

"It is small wonder that to most people, measurement and calculations like this do not seem to apply to the world they live in . . .," says Moss. "Underlying most talk of nuclear war is the phenomenon that Raymond Aron calls 'nuclear incredulity.' To most people, nuclear war does not seem to belong to the world of things that can really happen, like business troubles or school exams or next summer's holiday. More and more facts and more and more figures do not make it seem real."[20] In fact, more and more facts and figures probably make it seem less real. Certainly they deepen our psychic numbing: "The 'nuclear experts' serve a special function here, something on the order of hired anesthetists. They contribute to the numbing by further technicizing everything, by excluding human victims from their scenarios, and by conveying the sense that nuclear matters are completely under control because they are in the hands of experts."[21] Hence they foster that feeling of powerlessness whose attractions we have just explored.

However, we "leave it to the experts" not only out of numbed passivity, but also out of awe at their wizardlike expertise. Their technical language appears to be some sort of secret code, which only initiates in the mysteries can unravel. Moreover, these experts speak in numbers so large that they are effectively infinite. The creators of religious imagery throughout the world have known that huge numbers are powerful symbols of infinitude; hence we hear of billions of billions of trillions of Buddhas or the billions of billions of trillions of angels surrounding God's throne. These numbers are never meant to be taken literally but, rather, to inspire the awe and fascination with which we respond to the numinous mystery of infinitude. It is this same mystery that the nuclear strategists seem to have at their command. Thus, while the experts claim to speak in dispassionately rational language, they in fact create for the public a new and highly emotionally charged symbolic language—the language of rationally planned, technologically administered, abstract mass death. Here power and order meet in a truly awesome symbolism. Reason and unreason meet as well.

The confusion is compounded when the strategic theorists, while claiming to be totally dedicated to rational inquiry wherever it may lead, seeing their role as "to tamper, to change, to criticize," in fact speak totally within the framework of certain unquestioned ideological assumptions. Their reasoning may be flawless, but, as with all logical operations, the value of the results depends ultimately on the value of the axioms from which one begins. And in strategic analysis these axioms are usually the old symbolic statements that support and reflect the familiar ideological worldview; for example, that nuclear weapons are "here to stay" and therefore must be planned for rationally, that the "superpowers" are in an inevitable state of competition, that every nation-state wants to maximize its power, that MAD is an inevitable part of our nuclear policy, and so forth. If these assumptions were given dispassionate rational scrutiny, they might well prove to be questionable. But in the world of defense-intellectuals, only the "unrealistic" and "impractical" "utopian dreamers" dare to raise such questions.

From the 1960s on, a debate has raged on the subject of "thinking the unthinkable." Many argue that the work of Kahn and other strategists has in fact made nuclear war "thinkable," and therefore brought it closer to the realm of possibility merely because that possibility has been put into words. Kahn and his colleagues argue, of course, that merely denying the reality of a phenomenon by refusing to talk about it will not make it disappear. This seems to create an insoluble dilemma: both talking about nuclear war and refusing to talk about it lead equally to a greater likelihood of war.

But the dilemma may be more apparent than real, once we realize that the "experts" are prey to the same psychological mechanisms as everyone else—they are incapable of dealing with the new reality created by the Bomb in all of its overwhelming complexity, so they reduce it to language that appears new but is in fact fundamentally old and familiar. Hence their claim to face reality head-on masks their true unwillingness to do so. Their professional jargon, with its abstractions and technical terminology, is "a constellation of deception and self-deception that now dominates our world 'megamachine.' . . . One has to extricate oneself from the numbed language in order to begin to experience nuclear actuality."[22] If large numbers of people can extricate themselves from numbed language and talk about "nuclear actuality" as honestly as possible, their thought and discourse might prove to make nuclear war even less "thinkable" than it is now.

For the immediate future, however, the language of the defense strategists is likely to remain predominant. The general public will continue to experience the conflict between their symbolic perceptions of the Bomb and the experts' supposedly literal perception. At some level, though, the public may be dimly aware that the experts themselves are caught in a conflict between empirical and symbolic perceptions. Awareness of these conflicts, coupled with a realization that in the language of "techno-death" the human reality is completely effaced, produces a sense of discordant realities, which enhances the air of craziness surrounding the whole subject.

Yet the government, fostering nuclear armaments for a wide variety of reasons, willingly embraces the "experts," not only because elected officials feel unequipped to deal with the subject but also because the analysts' language offers the desired blend of symbolic impact and logical "realistic" appearance. Public statements by the government, often echoed by the media, of course will emphasize the ideological symbolic elements, indicating only that the impeccable logic of the experts supports the publicized conclusions. Thus the government's concern is not so much that the public understand the reasoning involved but, rather, that the public accept the prestige and mysterious wisdom of the experts. In other words, for the government the important thing is the analytic approach as a symbol, giving legitimation to its policies by creating a feeling of awe toward reasoning itself. Again, however, this symbolic dimension is insistently linked with the symbolic world created by the ideological assumptions, and those who question this symbolic structure are labeled "unrealistic" or, if need be, "crazy." Clearly the question of who is crazy is immensely complicated. As we try to unravel the intertwining strands of logic and illogic, reality and unreality, and literal and symbolic truth wrapped around the Bomb, the answer seems increasingly to be, "All of us."

But these paradoxes lead us back to the basic paradox of all religious experience: the same reality that threatens and terrifies us also lures us toward it, and for the very same reasons. Just as we are ambivalent about annihilation, so we are ambivalent about unreality and madness, for they too are the marks of the transcendence of limits. As our strange God, the machine that can only produce death, heightens the unreality and madness of the modern age because of its unique features, it simultaneously heightens our feelings of awe and fascination toward it. Moreover, these unique features create a reality in which reason imprisons us in the logic of annihilation; unreality and madness may become the most alluring of escapes. So, as we try to break out of the confines in which the Bomb has bound us, we depend upon the Bomb. Once again, the problem becomes its own solution.

5

THEATER OF
THE ABSURD

The problems that the Bomb claims to solve on the symbolic level are not all of its own making. The absurdities of technological rationality gone wild were already evident before Hiroshima—in Auschwitz and Dresden, in bureaucratic dehumanization, in mass starvation amid unprecedented luxury, in total war and totalitarian peace. The invention of nuclear weapons appears, from this perspective, to be merely the culmination of a process. As a dominating symbol of both our worldview and the craziness of life, the Bomb merely underscores the growing conviction that, despite the appearance of rationality, an absurd irrationality has in fact become the fundamental force in our world.

Yet this conviction may explain part of the positive appeal of nuclear weapons. For they have helped us to face this ever-mounting absurdity by suggesting that a world so deeply steeped in madness might not be real at all. Ill and evils that are unreal do not need to be confronted or coped with; a world that is unreal is actually easier to accept. More specifically, as we shall see in this chapter, the Bomb has eased our way by urging us to see itself, ourselves, and all of life as part of one great "play," both in the sense of theatrical spectacle and in the sense of a game to be played.

The key to this feeling lies in the supposedly literal discourse of the strategic analysts. In fact their language is riddled with metaphors, among the most important of which are the concepts of "scenario" and "nuclear theater." For these metaphors indicate that nuclear war can—perhaps must—be seen as a play in which the "actors" play out their roles in the scenario. Thus far the play has been most like a radio drama, for only the recitation of the words is involved; scripts are written by speech writers and recited by politicians in the appropriately theatrical settings. When a scenario is played out to its end, however, the actors must use actions as well as words to complete the script.

It is perhaps no accident that theatrical metaphors for war first became commonplace during World War I, the event that may be seen as the origin of the widespread sense of unreality and absurdity in modern Western culture. The analysis of theater language in that war, offered by Fussell, is highly relevant to the "nuclear theater" language as well: "The most obvious reason why 'theater' and modern war seem so compatible is that modern wars are fought by conscripted armies, whose members know they are only temporarily playing their ill-learned parts. . . . If 'real life' is 'real,' then military life must be pretense."[1] Of course, in the nuclear age there is no distinction between combatant and noncombatant—all are equally liable to destruction—and thus all are forced to play their ill-learned parts all the time.

Yet beyond the sense of being conscripted there is the unreality of the potential destruction itself. Fussell continues: "It is impossible for a participant to believe that he is taking part in such murderous proceedings in his own character. The whole thing is too grossly farcical, perverse, cruel, even absurd to be credited as a form of 'real life.' Seeing warfare as theater provides a psychic escape for the participant: with a sufficient sense of theater, he can perform his duties without implicating his 'real' self and without impairing his innermost conviction that the world is still a rational place."[2] But since the nuclear age forces us to be in the theater all the time, we must live as both actors and "real persons" simultaneously and permanently. This sense of watching oneself perform was pervasive during World War I: "Countless soldiers recall dividing into actor and audience at moments of the highest emergency."[3] It may be that in the nuclear age, life is constantly at a state of highest emergency, but in order to cope we must deny that reality by transforming ourselves into spectators of our own performance. Similarly, we are prepared to imagine ourselves as observers of global annihilation, ignoring the voice of reason, which tells us that we shall not be around to observe.

While World War I, with its fixed trenches and slow pace, was appropriately reflected in stage-play imagery, according to Fussell, World War II, "characterized by a new geographical remoteness, mobility, rapidity, complex technology, and ever-increasing incredibility,"[4] found its appropriate imagery in the language of film. He endorses Thomas Pynchon's identification of war with film; Pynchon "arrived almost at the final disclosure that modern life itself—equivalent, as his book has shown, to modern war—is a film too."[5] While media theorists might want to argue the fine points of nuclear war's affinities with live theater, film, and perhaps television, it is enough to point out here that twentieth-century war has pervasive links with the drama in all its forms.

But the implications of this go beyond war, particularly in an age when nuclear "trench warfare" is a constant reality. Bonnie Marranca writes: "The growth of the media and communications in the evolution of modern society has turned theatricalism into *the* 20th century political art form: it subsumes both ideology and individuality as our way of being in the contemporary world . . . , turning performance into a way of life."[6] While the "nuclear theater" in technical terms refers to the possibility of "limited" nuclear war outside of North America—making North Americans spectators— in a more general sense we are all participants in the ongoing drama. And it may be that the government stresses theatricalism as its primary political art form in order to keep us all feeling involved: "The most social of art forms, the form in which one experiences the representation of life in a space filled with living bodies, theater invites *participation*—which is what war psychology, when it mobilizes a country, is all about."[7]

It would be a mistake, however, to see the public as merely victims of government manipulation. For even more than participation, theater invites enjoyment—pleasure at seeing the spectacle unfold. Glenn Gray reflects on the "intense concentration on the spectacle" among soldiers in World War II: "Few of us can deny, if we are honest, a satisfaction in having seen them. . . . The major appeal in such spectacles . . . is the fascination that manifestations of power and magnitude hold for the human spirit. . . . He is lost in their majesty. His ego temporarily deserts him and he is absorbed into what he sees. An awareness of power that far surpasses his limited imagination transports him into a state of mind unknown in his everyday experiences."[8] The more intense the spectacle, then, the more fulfilling it is; and surely there is no more powerful spectacle imaginable than full-scale nuclear war.

For some of us, fascination with the Bomb may be merely the ultimate curiosity—a desire simply to witness ultimate power. Yet we know that we cannot just stand by and watch a nuclear war with avid curiosity; we must be involved in it. In Carey's study, a recurrent theme was "identification with this weird, all-powerful device, with the bomb itself. One's own 'craziness' joined that of the bomb, and fascination could extend to a wish that it be dropped so that one might witness this strange spectacle, experience the ultimate 'nuclear high,' and put an end to anxious wondering (and everything else, of course)."[9]

The theater of war has other appealing qualities as well. While scenarios and scripts are prepared in advance, there is always a large element of improvisation in this theater; the outcome remains in doubt, at least for a while, and thus it is a theater of suspense. Here the element of chance so appealing in gambling is combined with the power of the spectacle and the "human-interest appeal" of real characters relating to each other on the stage. This sense of suspense is particularly characteristic of nuclear war, with the built-in element of uncertainty, which is apparently a necessary feature of the MAD doctrine, for deterrence, writes Marranca, must involve "the ritualistic word play that purposely confuses intentionality, pretense, and uncertainty. The rhetorical drama that is at the heart of East-West relations is fueled by the role playing of masked superpower players whose dialogue has a frighteningly improvisational air about it. The thought that nuclear war might be a chance operation is overwhelming."[10] And the most overwhelming drama is the most intense, the most absorbing, ultimately the most enjoyable, particularly in an "audience-participation" show in which one is actor as well as observer. As the young student said, "It makes life more interesting."

The theater of nuclear war can be high drama, to be sure. The stakes are ultimate—deadly serious—and the tension of watching the plot unfold is gripping. Yet at times it seems that the play is not a drama at all but, rather, a comedy. And it is an appealing comedy, for it reflects the most popular comic form of our times—humor of the absurd. One can become a very successful comedian today by claiming to be "a wild and crazy guy." Behind this penchant for absurdist humor lies a deep-seated feeling that absurdity is the dominant quality of our world as a whole. Since there is inevitably a funny side to all craziness, one may as well laugh. It feels good to laugh, even when the humor is gallows humor. So the Bomb, as prime symbol of absurdity, becomes the prime symbol of humor of the absurd as well. The suggestion that the simplest solution to a given problem is to "nuke 'em" is invariably accompanied by a laugh. People are laughing at their own recognition of the absurdity of such a possibility, but also at the craziness of a world in which such a suggestion can be taken as a real possibility. It is ultimately the confusion over what is possible and what is impossible, what is real and what is unreal, that creates both the craziness and the humor that reflects it.

What could be more satisfying? The drama is highly charged, turns on Fate and Chance, involves cosmic issues and individual lives, brings unconscious fantasy to life, is tinged with comedy, and invites us to participate as both actors and audience. Yet all along we know that it is only theater, a play, not really real. And when the suspicion that this is rock-bottom reality creeps up on us, we have our facility of denial, or psychic numbing, to ease the pain and reassure us that there is really no danger. The Bomb is the symbol of this way of life.

It is not by chance that we call a theatrical production a "play." Our enjoyment of theater is possible because we can participate fully in every reality presented on the stage, secure in the knowledge that it is merely a "play," that the actors are merely "playing." And just as the theorists of nuclear strategy invite us to see nuclear war as "theater," so their language invites us equally to view it as a "game." "Game-theory" and the playing of "nuclear war games" are essential tools of their trade. To speak of the deaths of hundreds of millions of human beings in terms of "games" may sound like madness, no matter how much one protests that this is merely a technical term or an analytical device. Yet it fits quite smoothly into the pattern we have been sketching here. If the theatricality of nuclear war is appealing because it allows us to see that threat—and therefore life as a whole—as "unreal" and therefore enjoyable, how much more appealing to view it all as a game.

All games resemble theater in offering us a temporary escape from our ordinary world, an escape into a special world that combines power and intensity with rules and structure. We enjoy these worlds because they offer us relief from both the boredom and the tensions of our day-to-day lives. Yet we are glad they are only "games," so that when the intensity becomes too much to bear we need merely walk away. However, modern students of "play" as a dimension of human culture have shown us how hard it is to separate "play" from "real life"; it seems clear that the nuclear age has made it much harder, perhaps impossible. Again, the dual role of player and spectator is crucial here. When the game seems enjoyable and interesting, one perceives oneself as player. But when it becomes too overwhelming and one no longer wants to play, one conveniently switches to the role of spectator—unable to influence the outcome, and therefore a mere victim of Fate or Chance.

When the "play," be it game or theater, involves awesome unlimited power and sacred structures, it becomes religious ritual. Ritual is, in a sense, a play of utmost solemnity, a play that follows a carefully written scenario with perfect fidelity. In ritual, "intense religious emotion is accompanied by a performance that is known to be artificial, a spectacle that is knowingly played but that is in no way meant to be deception or diversion. . . . The ritual order is a mere convention. In the profane world, it delimits a separate area ruled by a strict code."[11]

From this perspective, it is easy to understand that war has often been a central form of ritual, and hence of play: It has its "strict code," and it may be entered into not to gain some extrinsic end but for the intrinsic value of playing the game. However, says Aho:

> It must not be thought that if warfare is a game, then the players are allowed to proceed in an attitude of hilarity and nonseriousness. . . . For the Romans, Hindus, Germans, and Chinese to consider war a form of play was to count it among the most solemn and significant of man's affairs. For above all,

unlike its antithesis "work," "play" refers to those activities engaged in as ends in themselves. Play is not some "servile" art whose value is found in its utility relative to ends apart from itself. On the contrary, it is the essence of sacred liturgy, the ritual celebration of the highest ends.[12]

War, then, may resemble rituals, games, and plays both in being taken with utmost seriousness and in containing an obvious dimension of unreality. The attractive side of this unreality is apparent in the case of games and plays; Jonathan Z. Smith has suggested that a similar dynamic may be at work in much religious activity. He posits that there may be two fundamentally different types of human cultures. Some stress the congruence between reality and the symbols, myths, and rituals that are believed to reflect reality; they affirm that there is an overarching unity and coherence throughout the universe, a unity that is adequately mirrored in their religious symbols. But other cultures accept, and even emphasize, the fact that symbols, myths, and rituals are abstractions and thus different from the reality they reflect. They are, in a sense, finite blueprints or schematic diagrams for a reality that is infinite, and thus there must be divergences between diagram and reality.

In these latter cultures, the very unreality of symbols, and the myths and rituals built from them, is experienced as a powerful and fascinating facet of life. People "play" with the complexity of both "fit" and "lack of fit" between symbol and reality and find power and pleasure in this "play." Thus the Bomb as a symbol, as a central focus in our mythic worldview and ritualized behavior, may derive its power in part from its congruence with the worldview but also in part from its incongruity. Perceiving the unreality that surrounds the Bomb may enhance its sense of power and therefore its appeal for us.

But religious activity also resembles modern theater by incorporating an element of absurdity, which is experienced as humorous. To "play" on incongruity can be funny and fun. In Smith's words:

There is something funny, there is something crazy about myth for it shares with the comic and the insane the quality of obsessiveness. Nothing, in principle, is allowed to elude its grasp. . . . Myth shares with other forms of human speech such as the joke or riddle, a perception of a possible relationship between different "things." It delights, it gains its power, knowledge and value from the play between. . . . It is precisely the juxtaposition, the incongruity between the expectation and the actuality that serves as a vehicle of religious experience.[13]

The absurd unreality of war, and especially of nuclear war, may evoke the same kinds of responses that Smith finds in these religious phenomena. If the Bomb is our primary access to this kind of "play" today, we may be reluctant to part with it. And the pleasure in this "play" may be related to the Bomb's role as symbol of both power and structure, and our ambivalence toward these. In the "play" of unreality we can find power in lack of structure and a light, playful dimension in structure and power. Thus we are able to act out and accept our ambivalence. In doing so, however, we are forced to deal with reality as if it were in some sense unreal, while we deal with unreality as if it were profoundly real. Perhaps the Bomb has aided us, or even compelled us, to turn our world into such a theater of the absurd in which all of life becomes a ritualized playfulness.

The feeling of unreality generated by nuclear weapons reaches its culmination, however, when one goes past the sense of living in an absurdist play and arrives at the conviction that, if all of this can't be real, it must be a dream. One victim of Hiroshima described the long lines of his fellow residents streaming out of the city, "so broken and confused that they moved and behaved like automatons," as "the exodus of a people who walked in the realm of dreams."[14] But the dream is hardly a pleasant one. Its surrealism and terror can only be matched by the worst of nightmares: "Nagasaki destroyed by the magic of science is the nearest man has yet approached to the realization of dreams that even during the safe immobility of sleep are accustomed to develop into nightmares of anxiety. The first promise of the atomic age is that it can make some of our nightmares come true. The capacity so painfully acquired by normal men to distinguish between sleep, delusion, hallucination and the objective reality of waking life has for the first time in human history been seriously weakened."[15]

The nightmare terrifies us not only because of what we suffer in it, but also because of the suffering we inflict on ourselves and others. In the nuclear age, "as when we dream, we are both the authors and sufferers of our fate . . . ," writes Schell. "We don't want to face the fact that we are potential mass killers."[16] Yet our possession of the Bomb compels us to face this reality, which was previously repressed in the depths of the unconscious: "If we take a look at dreams, we note that war is endemic in our unconscious. Every one of us carries within himself silent, secret murders. . . . Now the technico-cultural progress has translated the fantasies of omnipotent sadistic control into nuclear weapons as concrete destructive omnipotence. Nuclear weapons have always existed in the unconscious of human individuals in the form of concrete destructive intent" (Fornari).[17] If we feel powerless to prevent the realization of our nightmare fears of annihilation, we may feel equally powerless to prevent the realization of our fears of annihilating others as well.

It all seems crazy: we don't want to be annihilated, nor do we want to annihilate others. We don't want to be in this situation, yet there seems to be no way out. We are hemmed in on every side by paradox. As soon as we begin thinking seriously about this reality, we are plunged into the kinds of distortions of reason that are supposed to occur only in dreams. And when one wants to escape from a dream but can't, it is a nightmare. Yet perhaps there is no great desire to escape. The same factors that make it congenial to see life as unreal, as theater, also make it equally acceptable to see it all as a dream. "Life is but a dream" has been a comforting thought in many cultures, and perhaps today, given our need to deny the reality in which we live, it may be more comforting than ever. For if thinking about nuclear weapons is nightmarish, then it must be admitted that nightmares don't occur all that often. They pass as quickly as they come, and we return to more peaceful and even pleasant dreams. Nor are we helpless to make them pass; our facility to deny and to numb ourselves is of immeasurable help here. Living on two levels, we need only experience the nightmare level on rare occasions, and when it becomes too painful we force ourselves to switch to the "ordinary-life" level of tolerable dreaming. But none of it need be accepted as "real."

Modern psychology has persuaded us, of course, that dreams are just as "real" as waking life, since they embody a reality that the dreamer carries around all the time, albeit unconsciously. Religious traditions have expressed this same truth of the "reality" of dreams in many ways. Dreams are always held to have power of some sort, and great power is seen in those who can negotiate in "reality" the realm that the average person meets only in dreams. Such persons—shamans, prophets, soothsayers—give form and substance to the dream world, in the view of modern psychology, and allow it to become a substantial part of the waking world; hence their special power and prestige. It would seem that the distinction between dream world and waking world is a limitation that human beings accept with a certain frustration. There is satisfaction in blurring, or even eliminating, the distinction, in living our dreams and fantasies: "Make your dreams come true" has perennial appeal. If there is a necessary conflict between conscious and unconscious dimensions of thought and feeling, as some psychologies hold, then we can well understand the appeal of erasing the difference. There is thus good reason to believe that life as dream—like life as theater—is an appealing possibility, and again the Bomb serves as symbol and chief support for access to this realm.

Here, as in so many symbolic dimensions of nuclear weapons, we are again deeply ambivalent. The thought that life is unreal is, like the Bomb itself, awesome, inspiring both horror and fascination, repulsion and attraction. This ambivalence is deepened by awareness that the most pleasant moments of theater and dream can quickly turn into absurdist nightmare. Thus our nuclear arsenals afford us the luxury and condemn us to the terror of living in a dream world of unreal reality. But they do so only so long as they sit in their silos unused. "Those who dream of a great feast may weep the next morning. Those who dream of weeping may enjoy the hunt the next day. While they dream, they do not know they are dreaming. They may even interpret their dreams while still dreaming. Only after they awake do they know it was a dream. By and by, there will be a great awakening; then we will know that this is all a great dream."[18]

6

THE MYTH OF
THE HERO

This is an appropriate point at which to pause, summarize, and get our bearings. The first chapter suggested that the Bomb has taken the place of our ancestors' God as our prime symbol of limitlessness. Therefore it arouses deep ambivalence; there is fascination as well as fear of the prospect of annihilation. The second chapter related both fear and fascination to our desire for a sacred structure rooted in limitless reality—an order that embraces both duality and unity. The third chapter spoke of the appeal of fatalism when structure grows rigid; then it turned to the disordered side of limitlessness and showed how this breeds a fascination with chance. The fourth and fifth chapters continued the discussion of the disordered and the irrational, as reflected in the Bomb's symbolisms of unreality, madness, and absurdity.

It has been clear throughout that our ambivalence is a response to both sides of the coin of infinitude: just as we both fear and long for its chaotic side, so we both long for and fear its orderly, comprehensible side. We accept the fear, perhaps even cherish it, because we recognize it as a necessary element in our relationship to the unlimited. And what we desire, above all, is a transcendence of our limits. As our forebears sought this goal through one awesome omnipotent God, so we seek it through one awesome omnipotent weapon.

Now we shall turn to another fundamental dimension of the ambivalent quest for transcendence. Of all the limits that weigh upon humanity, surely none is as heavy as the inevitability of death.

84

Behind every threat of chaos and destruction lurks the ever-present possibility of our own death. Death is at the center of that constellation of irrationality, unreality, and absurdity that we have been examining. Death is also at the center of our fear and fascination with the Bomb. If the release we seek is ultimately a release from death, then our goal is not simply eternity and omnipotence but the guarantee of more life. And the security we seek is an order that can support and nourish life forever. But just as we are drawn to the life-destroying power of the Bomb, so we are fascinated by the unknown terror of death.

Both life and death are expressions of the one limitless reality, and religious experience must see them as a unity. All of the ambivalences we have discovered thus far are in one sense facets of our deep ambivalence toward this most profound unity. But focusing on the dimension of life and death shows us a resolution of this ambivalence: when we pass through chaos to new order— through death to new life—we satisfy our longing to transcend limits without paying the ultimate price. We accept the lure of annihilation, only to discover that it is a temporary condition, a gateway to renewal and rebirth. This is perhaps the most pervasive theme in all the world's religious myth and ritual. It may also be the most pervasive theme in the symbolism of nuclear weapons.

The logic underlying the religious view of death has already been suggested in the first chapter. Annihilation, as an escape from all limits, releases new power and effects a transcendence to a higher state of being. On the individual level, this is experienced as an initiation into a new mode of reality. In puberty rites, healing ceremonies, funerals, mystical initiations—wherever one's status is radically transformed—the message of both myth and ritual is that the new cannot be born unless the old willingly dies. Communities embrace this message too. In the festival, as we noted, there is a return to the primal chaos; this preexistent state is often equated with death, yet it is enthusiastically embraced not only for the intrinsic value of release but also for the repetition of creation that is sure to follow. And as the religious community renews itself, its recitation of the creation myth seems to say that the whole world is dying, returning to its primordial darkness, so that it can be born again.

It is not surprising that victims of the Hiroshima bombing felt the whole world dying: "My body seemed black, everything seemed dark, dark all over. . . . Then I thought, 'The world is ending.' . . . I thought this was the end of Hiroshima—of Japan—of mankind. . . . I thought it might have been something which had nothing to do with the war, the collapse of the earth which it was said would take place at the end of the world."[1] It is surprising, though, that some *hibakusha* could later find the possibility of new life rising out of the ashes: "When the war ended as a result of the A-bomb . . . we found something to live for. . . . The disaster was horrible, but through it we felt a new meaning in life."[2] But Lifton found that many survivors, in order to cope with their experience, needed some symbolism of rebirth; to evoke these symbols, they spontaneously drew on the mind's potential for mythological thinking.[3]

The same potential was also triggered among those who dropped the Bomb. Much of America's response to the first atomic bombs was shaped by the reporting of journalist William Laurence. Laurence, having watched the first nuclear explosion, wrote: "One felt as though he had been privileged to witness the Birth of the World. . . . The big boom came about a hundred seconds after the great flash—the first cry of the newborn world. . . . If the first man could have been present at the moment of Creation when God said, 'Let there be light,' he might have seen something very similar to what we have seen."[4] Lifton has noted that many who were professionally involved with nuclear weapons were grasped by a religious fascination with the "new technological deity . . . seen as capable not only of apocalyptic destruction but also of unlimited creation."[5] The crucial point in such a religious view, of course, is that destruction is the necessary prelude to creation and therefore a consummation devoutly, albeit fearfully, to be wished.

If this kind of mythological imagery was a common response to bombs dropped in the past, it is even more common in responding to bombs that might fall in the future. Perhaps this is inevitable. In order to think about a nuclear war at all, as we have seen, the mind is compelled to put itself in the role of survivor. It is compelled to assume that something must follow cataclysmic destruction, and so it finds itself willy-nilly in the age-old scenario of death and rebirth. Nuclear war easily comes to appear, especially in unconscious fantasy, as the "big bang" that will wipe away the accumulated terrors of history and bring the birth of a pristine new world. The Bomb therefore comes to symbolize the endlessness of the chain of death-and-life, playing the role of destroyer and creator that was once reserved for a less technological deity.

The inescapable lure of this mythic pattern is surely evident in the myriad fictional nuclear wars that have filled literature, television, film, and comic books for forty years. In these science-fiction depictions, there is always at least a hint—and often much more than a hint—that annihilation is acceptable, or even desirable, as the necessary prelude to new creation.

The appeal of science fiction, like the appeal of myth, comes in part from the very act of experiencing the story. As reader or listener or viewer, one is taken out of the normal everyday world and projected into a "fabulous" time, in which the events are more powerful, more intense, more grandiose than any we have actually known. Thus the world of myth and science fiction is "surreal"— more than real. Yet at the same time it is, in the modern view, unreal, as in our characteristic equation of "mythical" with "unreal." But this, too, as we have seen, is a consolation and even an attraction when speaking of nuclear weapons; by casting them into an unreal setting we can make our own world with its precariousness and all-enveloping danger unreal as well. Thus mythicizing can make nuclear war more appealing, while the terrible danger of nuclear war makes the mythicizing of it more appealing as well. Just as we are ambivalent about the dangers of nuclear war, so are we ambivalent about the powers spoken of in myth.

But the appeal of a mythicized imaginary nuclear war as depicted in science fiction rests as much or more on the content of that fiction as on the form. The most pervasive story about nuclear war in all science fiction is that which might be called "the myth of the heroic survivors." The plot is familiar enough to need no specific documentation: despite the vast destruction, some do survive. They are the characters in the story, the "real" people with whom we are to identify. They are usually more blond and beautiful and creative and capable than we are, but not more than we imagine ourselves to be or think we deserve to be. After an appropriately brief glance backward at the destruction of their civilization, they begin to build a new civilization—a new human future which is inevitably better than the human past.

The actual situation after a nuclear war might, of course, bear little if any resemblance to this mythic vision. But such logical objections are unlikely to diminish its attractiveness. For this scenario speaks not to the logical mind but to the unconscious yearning in each of us to be a hero. The myth of the heroic survivors of nuclear war is merely one instance of the more general myth of the hero, which is perennially popular in our culture as in every other. In one form or another, it is the mainstay of all of our popular entertainments. The hero myth appeals primarily because it exemplifies the theme of death and rebirth in the life of a single individual, an individual with whom we can identify; thus we can vicariously experience death and rebirth ourselves. In experiencing ordeals, battles, tests of strength, suffering, and the like, the hero is actually undergoing a symbolic death, thereby escaping from the world with its temporality and history. Like the community that recites and reenacts its myths, the hero symbolically returns to the beginning and is reborn as a new being, replicating the birth of the world out of chaos; and he thereby experiences a new, fresh cosmos, cleansed of the accumulated terrors and sufferings of past history. The hero is initiated and raised to a higher spiritual level, learning the sacred wisdom that is reserved for initiates alone.

The heroic survivors of science-fiction nuclear war are classic initiates, for they are in fact on a higher level—their world is more intense, more "real," and life is experienced on a cosmic scale—while they have also gained a certain kind of mature wisdom, which, along with the new technical skills they acquire, enables them to forge a new and better life for themselves and their descendants. They have experienced the primordial chaos, the escape from time, and are reborn in a timeless world; having survived total death, they need no longer fear death and thus no longer fear time. The myth of the hero and the initiatory scenario have offered a sense of hope on a cosmic scale to millennia of human beings, and there is little reason to think that they have ceased to do so now.

The heroic-survivor plot does not always appear in such a pristine form. There are innumerable possible variants, of which some are particularly interesting. One, for example, reflects that particularly American version of the hero myth that has been called the "Captain America complex." In this variant, the common people, with whom we identify, are left helpless in the face of the catastrophe that they have just survived. But an all-powerful stranger (Captain America, Superman, the Lone Ranger) arrives unexpectedly on the scene, sets the situation right, and then leaves as abruptly as he came, with the mystery of his identity still unsolved. This stranger may be a technological genius who provides the knowledge needed to build the new civilization. Alternatively, the unknown hero may be an inscrutable "wise man" who gives the survivors the wisdom to rebuild their world in a more peaceful and humane—though often less highly technologized—way. In either event, the myth is attractive because we ourselves are just as likely as not to be among the happy survivors, chosen by Fate or Chance, who need expend no effort to gain and enjoy a reborn world.

A related mythic plot, though in a different context, involves the hero who saves the nation or the world on the brink of nuclear disaster. While this myth does not speak of actual dissolution and rebirth, it does reflect the myth of the hero because the hero often confronts mortal danger but averts it. Here, as in the "Captain America" myth, the common people are helpless and must rely on a lone individual with special technological or other abilities to rescue them at the last moment from imminent destruction. Again, this myth is satisfying in part because we identify with the hero and in part because we identify with the helpless but ultimately safe masses whom the hero rescues. While the other myths discussed here promote an unrealistic sense of the reality of nuclear war, this myth promotes an equally unrealistic sense of the reality of nuclear weapons, affording us the luxury of believing that we shall always be pulled back from the brink and thus have nothing to fear. The appeal of this sense of unreality, this perception of nuclear weapons as theatrical props, is certainly part of the appeal of this mythical approach to the subject. For if nuclear weapons and war are mythical, then perhaps all of our lives are mythical, and there is fascination (as well as terror) in living in the intensity, power, and drama of myth. Moreover, as we have seen, there may be equal fascination in exploring the contradiction between myth and reality; hence the mythic approach, whether believed to be "realistic" or not, can generate a power that attracts us to it.

Even some of the variants that stress the difficulties of surviving a nuclear war may contain important attractive elements. In some plots, the survivors must face a continuing series of smaller crises after surviving the initial catastrophe. Yet in most cases the survivors experience these lesser crises as a series of new initiations—new chances to experience the joys of rebirth and learn new skills that are necessary in rebuilding the world. In even more pessimistic visions, the survivors are unable to restore anything of the culture that has been destroyed; their lives become so degraded that they seem to be almost subhuman. We can often find in this plot a reversion to the "natural" or even animal state. Yet such a reversion forms a positive element in many myths that oppose the simple joys of nature to the tortured artifices of civilization.

Civilization itself is often experienced as a complex set of limitations, and there is a pervasive desire to experience the organic wholeness and spontaneity that we attribute to the animal world and, in general, to nature. Hence the popular appeal of wilderness, the "great out-of-doors"—which has been increasing in recent years—the fantasy of living off the land, the fascination with the "wild child" raised solely by animals, and so forth. Among the many symbolic meanings of nuclear weapons, one of the most widespread and often heard is their ability to "wipe out the whole mess so we can start over again." One college student wrote: "I have sometimes thought that massive human destruction by nuclear war may be the social means by which evolution is working its course to re-establish a balance which we have thrown askew."[6] It is crucial to note, of course, that when profound pessimism with the state of civilization leads to such a wish, there is always the assumption that if "*we* wipe out the whole mess, *we* can start over again"; the advocates of such a solution always assume their own survival. Thus even when fiction writers hope to portray a totally negative view of nuclear war, the popular imagination may well turn that view into something positive and attractive.

7

THE APOCALYPTIC VISION

In the history of Western civilization, perhaps the most potent and influential version of the myth of heroic survival has been the tradition of the apocalypse. Since the writings of Albert Schweitzer on the subject, scholars have been increasingly persuaded that the apocalypse is the foundation on which Christianity was built, and it has been a basic element in Christianity, although its influence waxed and waned in different times and places. The apocalypse has also been a fundamental formative influence in Judaism and Islam, but it may be of great importance to note that nuclear weapons have been developed and deployed first by nations shaped pervasively by Christian backgrounds, and the spread of nuclear weapons has been part of the spread of a Western civilization that is primarily Christian in orientation. (The Christian tradition has probably been nearly as influential in Russia, despite its official disestablishment since 1917, as it has in other Western lands.) The apocalyptic orientation, as we shall see, bears upon the symbolic meaning of nuclear weapons in a number of ways.

The basic notions of an apocalyptic viewpoint are fairly easily understood. It involves the belief that there is a God who is ultimately guiding the historical process from the creation of the world to some final end or consummation. Human beings are free to choose whether to support this God, obeying and advancing his will, or to oppose him, but the essential course of history is fixed by God. The course of history is basically one in which God allows his opponents to gain the upper hand temporarily in political, economic, and social domination of the world. At a certain time, this situation will be radically reversed. There will be a cataclysmic change, usually said to involve some kind of violence, and the supporters of God will become the rulers, or even the sole survivors. God's opponents will finally receive the punishment, or even total destruction, that they deserve for having chosen opposition. Apocalyptic traditions often, though not always, include the assertion that the time of radical reversal is imminent or even presently under way, and there is usually a claim that this knowledge, as well as the understanding of the whole historical process, comes from some sort of secret wisdom provided by God to an apocalyptic prophet or visionary.

In this basic apocalyptic orientation a number of themes are already familiar from our analysis of the symbolism of nuclear weapons. There is the claim that a single power is at the heart of all reality, from beginning to end. There is a sense of fatalism—that the essence of the historical process is beyond one's ability to change. There is an overriding perception of dualism; all humanity is divided into the "good" people and the "evil" who oppose them. In the apocalyptic cataclysm, there is a return to the primordial chaos, a destruction cosmic in scale that wipes out the dominance of "evil" once and for all. This return to chaos provides the "clean slate" that allows for a new birth—a new world in which the "good" will take their rightful place as masters or even sole occupants. There is a feeling that one is now living in the time of the end, that one is already feeling the pervasive effects of a worldwide annihilation, which may be fully manifest at any moment. Yet, if one is convinced of being on the "good" side, this annihilation is actually to be welcomed, for it offers a sense of security that is otherwise unavailable. The new situation about to be created will be an eternal one; the ability of "evil" to harm the "good" will be permanently destroyed. Thus the "good" will enjoy a permanence of security and tranquillity that was previously unavailable to them. Finally, this apocalyptic truth, like the truth behind nuclear weapons, is a secret one, which is available only to a chosen few who can then spread the good news to the rest of their community.

A brief look at the historical development of apocalyptic traditions shows even more direct links between that view of the world and the significance of nuclear arms. Apocalyptic seems to have been born among people in ancient Israel who believed that they were being denied the leadership role that was their right. These first apocalyptists believed that they had a mandate from God to rule the Israelite people, but they found themselves out of power because a politically stronger group had usurped their rightful place. Thus they were faced with what psychologists call "cognitive dissonance." They were forced to accept two mutually contradictory truths: one, that the all-powerful God wanted them to rule, and the other, that they were not in fact ruling despite God's omnipotence. In order to avoid denying either of these truths, they developed the idea that God did indeed intend for them to rule, but not yet. God had allowed the usurpers to gain temporary control; clearly, if the usurpers had control and God was omnipotent, then God must have allowed them to obtain that control. A central conclusion from all this was that God works in mysterious ways. He allows the human situation to get worse and worse, until he finally intercedes to transform it radically. When God does intercede, he appears as a mighty warrior, setting the world right through violent punishment of "evil." Thus the end of this age was often pictured in terms of battle imagery.

While this early apocalyptic originated in Israelite religion, its basic features can be traced back to Canaanite religion. The image of God as warrior, so fundamental throughout Western history, seems to go back to strikingly similar images of the Canaanite deities El and Baal as warriors. Throughout the world, the enemy of the warrior god is typically, as in Canaan and Israel, the enemy of human life: death and disorder, on the natural level (famine, drought, earthquake, flood) and on the social level (injustice, oppression, crime). The god must fight actively against the (usually personified) force of disorder and death. Yet in Canaan, as in so many cultures, that "evil" force must be given its due. It cannot be suppressed completely, once and for all. Its defeat is temporary; it returns and wins victories itself, thus requiring that the warrior god return to fight another battle to end the temporary rule of evil. Each time the warrior god is temporarily eclipsed but wins out in the end, he repeats the heroic initiatory scenario of death and rebirth, and the human beings who hear or recite or act out his exploits experience that death and rebirth as well. The inevitable moments of disorder in human life—drought, flood, oppression, disease, death—come to be interpreted in terms of this mythic cycle and therefore receive an ultimately positive value as the prerequisite for a new birth, a new victory of good over evil.

While there are highly significant differences between the Israelite and Canaanite phenomena, there are very important continuities as well. The warrior God in both cases appears to set things right, to end the disorder of injustice and oppression, and ultimately to bring life to the world, for life cannot flourish when injustice rules. For the ancients (and perhaps for moderns in some ways too) order in the natural realm and order in the social realm were inextricably tied together; neither could flourish without the other. Yet order could not be produced until the existing situation of disorder had been completely dissolved. But total dissolution means total disorder; thus disorder had to be allowed to prevail completely for at least a moment, so that a new, perfect order could be born out of it. In Israelite apocalyptic, of course, the omnipotent God could not himself be defeated by disorder. But his people could be defeated, and they could be engulfed by the catastrophe of total war between good and evil, war on both a human and a cosmic scale.

War itself thus comes to be a prime symbol of the temporary intensification of disorder, the rule of evil. Yet simultaneously, war appears in this context as a positive and necessary phenomenon, for it prepares the way for perfect and eternal peace. In this way the problem of cognitive dissonance is solved. When the good see evil prevail, they understand that this is a necessary stage in the pattern of world history, that God in a sense has no choice but to allow the rule of evil to engulf the world so that the final battle may be fought when both good and evil have reached their highest pitch of power. In this light, the final battle appears as the most intense experience of power imaginable, and it is a release of limitless power, which serves to repair and reaffirm cosmic and social order and instate them eternally as unshakable structures. Because the rule of evil is thus serving God's purpose, it in no way compromises or challenges his omnipotence. To participate in the historical process that leads to cataclysmic war is thus to participate in the power of God and share in the establishment of permanent order.

The apocalyptic worldview had reached a preeminent and pervasive role in Jewish life in Palestine when Jesus appeared. By that time, an important place in the apocalyptic scenario was accorded to a human figure who would be God's special agent—his "anointed one" or Messiah—and, in many versions of the tradition, the leader of his human armies in the final battle. This Messiah would lead God's people to victory over evil and would become the king of the newly born perfect world of order and peace. Scholars will probably dispute endlessly the precise ways in which perceptions of Jesus agreed with or differed from Jewish beliefs about the Messiah, but a few general points seem fairly obvious.

The earliest believers in Jesus may well have been faced with a cognitive dissonance of their own. On the one hand, they believed Jesus to be in some way a possessor of divine powers and thus a human representation of omnipotence. On the other hand, they knew that he had been subjected to Roman power in the most drastic way—he had been put to death and thus shown to be as powerless as any other mortal. Was it God who was omnipotent or the Roman emperor? The solution to this problem was a new application of the basic apocalyptic insight going back to Canaanite times. Jesus, like the warrior god of Canaan, must be defeated temporarily so that the world can reach the full intensity of dissolution. But it was equally certain that when the situation had reached rock bottom Jesus would return again "in power" to manifest himself as the savior of the good. Thus in the person of Jesus salvation had already been manifest on earth; the decisive battle had already been fought. Even though to mere human eyes it seemed as though the battle had been lost—the savior had been crucified—those who knew the secret of the good news knew that the truth was quite the opposite. The crucifixion was, rather, a guarantee that the savior was victorious.

As in any long war, there is still much fighting to be done after the decisive battle. The losing side may appear to gain further victories, but these victories are ultimately meaningless because the outcome has been determined. Thus those on the side that wins the decisive battle must keep fighting, but they really have nothing to fear. Even if they should lose their lives, they know that they do so in a winning cause. Many scholars believe that essentially this view dominated early Christianity. Even if one had to endure the terrible wars and catastrophes predicted for the last days in the book of Revelation, they could be welcomed as the inevitable accompaniments of the birth of a new, perfect world.

Of course, as time went on and the end did not come, there was a relaxation of apocalyptic tensions among many Christians. The Church had to build structures and institutions that would endure in this unredeemed world. Yet there was always the conviction that in some way all of this was part of the end, an end which might take an unpredictably long time to be fully manifest but which had already started in the time of Jesus. Thus Christianity prepared its adherents to accept war and all other adversity as a necessary part of the intensification of evil, which must take place during the end, just as Jesus had provided the model by accepting his death on the cross. And the seeds of an intense apocalypticism were always there, ready to flower when conditions were right. The conditions were usually the same as those that had given birth to apocalyptic: a sense of fundamental wrong and disorder, a sense that one's rightful place in the world-order had been abridged or usurped and thus the world-order itself thrown out of joint. While outright oppression and injustice could easily evoke such a feeling, it could also come from more subtle causes.

In times of rapid social change, when accustomed styles of life and social structures were likely to break down, those who saw no advantage in the change or were otherwise unwilling to embrace the change often suffered from cognitive dissonance. On the one hand, they knew that things "ought" to be a certain way for they had apparently always been that way, and it felt "right" for them to be that way. On the other hand, it was apparent from looking at the world that things were no longer the way they "ought" to be: things had changed. And when lifestyles and social structures change, the symbols on which they are built and which give them power also change. Those who cling to the old symbols often find themselves bewildered and powerless, for power tends to gravitate to those who can successfully negotiate (and manipulate) the new powerful symbols.

As a solution to cognitive dissonance and powerlessness, many will try to align themselves with what they see as the enduring source of power. If they are Christians, they will turn to God, the apocalyptic redeemer, to find both a sense of permanence and an answer to their dissonance—an answer that assures them that they will ultimately have total power. Knowing that they are among the good, the "elect," they know that the final outcome will be to their advantage, no matter how horrendous the process by which it comes about. They are destined to be heroic survivors, to die and be reborn as the world dies and is reborn.

The links between apocalyptic and modern attitudes toward nuclear war are obvious enough. In some communities there is a direct link explicitly articulated between God's power, the nation's power as embodied in its nuclear arsenal, the Christian community's power, and the individual's power. Such communities tend (though it is important not to overgeneralize here) to stress the value of traditional structures and lifestyles and the symbols that support and embody them, thus rejecting the rapid change that they see around them. It is not surprising that a president who came to power promising a return to traditional values was also perceived as more willing to brandish the nuclear sword against the nation's supposed enemies. But the appeal of apocalyptically influenced attitudes may well be wider than the circle of explicitly apocalyptically oriented Christian communities.

Perhaps the one feature of modern life that everyone can agree on—whether endorsing, opposing, or merely acquiescing—is the extraordinary rapidity of change. As technological and social and economic forms change, the symbols that express them must change too. Such a process may easily become intolerable to the psyche. When it does, there is an understandable desire to stop the process, to fix the structure and its symbols once and for all. This in turn may easily become a fanatic dedication to one's own symbols and a demand that everyone accept these particular symbols. Carried to extremes, this results in a kind of "totalism," which is at the heart of modern fascism. And fascism clearly has roots in the apocalyptic tradition; it is willing to provoke worldwide conflict and catastrophe, if need be, secure in the trust that "our side" will inevitably emerge victorious and the "other side," embodying total evil, will be eliminated, thus purifying the world for future generations.

There are few people who can be totally open to constant change. In most of us there is at least some degree of desire for permanence, for an enduring and dependable world of structures and symbols. Thus most of us have some capacity to be drawn toward a "totalizing" apocalypticlike orientation, identifying the familiar with the good and the unfamiliar with the evil. Moreover, rapid change is likely to affect us all in some adverse ways, and thus many will be predisposed to feel victimized in some way or another, and this too lends itself to apocalyptic attitudes in which the victims eagerly await the reversal of roles. But even those whose personal situation does not dispose them at all toward apocalypticism cannot entirely escape its influence. Because apocalyptic is so central in Christianity, it is necessarily a central element in Western civilization. No one raised in a Western culture can remain untouched by this view of history. It is hardly coincidental that *Star Wars*, with its simplistic apocalyptic plot, was the most popular film of our time.

Although other interpretations of history are certainly available and have been important in various ways, none has been quite as influential as the apocalyptic. This means that when Westerners want to appropriate the myth of the hero or the initiatory scenario of death and rebirth in a personally meaningful way, they are led almost inevitably to look to the historical process. And when Westerners want to relate to history in a meaningful way, the apocalyptic scenario will almost inevitably be present. This was as true of Karl Marx, despite his desire to eliminate traditional religion, as it was of the American founding fathers and the Nazis, each of whom drew in their own ways on this basic stock of traditions. For one of the distinctive features of Western culture is that, absorbing some of the fundamentals of Christianity, it also necessarily absorbed fundamentals of biblical Israelite religion. And perhaps the key to the latter is that, in appropriating the Canaanite religion, it took a mythological process of death and rebirth and read it into the historical process; it fused myth and politico-social history. Thus the divine warrior must act in the historical process; the disorder that he overcomes is fundamentally political disorder.

The great innovation of ancient Israelite religion was its drive to see everything in terms of the God who acts in, on, and through the processes of human political life. Thus it became impossible to separate mythic perceptions from perceptions of the political history of the nation. "Evil" as a mythological reality was fused with the real political enemies of Israel, domestic and foreign. And the mythological dissolution, which prepared the way for spiritual or cosmic rebirth, was fused with the real military wars, which prepared the way for a reestablishment of peace and the political order. Although this fusion of myth and politics is not as pervasive in Christianity, it is nevertheless an indelible part of Christianity's foundation. Westerners are inevitably drawn to seeing political conflict in terms of the apocalyptic scenario, even when their reason or better judgment warns against it.

This tendency has been significantly magnified by the development of nuclear weapons. In times past the temptation to go to war has always been fostered in part by the sense that this might be the final war, the war to end all wars. Now, for the first time, the apocalyptic vision of a final war—a cataclysmic destruction of cosmic proportions—is truly within humanity's ability to realize. The power that would be released when good and evil reach their fullest intensity and collide is the awesome power of the atom. With its 2,000-year history of apocalypticism, convinced that the end is now and the victory of "our side" is inevitable, with just one final battle needed to rid the world of evil forever, it is hardly surprising that the Christian West is loath to give up its nuclear weapons.

In sum, the appeal of apocalyptic embodies a number of factors that reinforce each other: It is ingrained in our culture. It makes sense out of the contradictions that appear in times of rapid change. It gives the myth of death and rebirth an especially vivid sense of reality by projecting it into the politico-historical process. It ties together many of the appealing aspects of the symbolism of nuclear weapons that we have discussed here. And it simplifies and solidifies the worldview, neatly separating good and evil and stressing the inevitability of the victory of good.

There is, however, one important way in which the apocalyptic view cannot be applied to the nuclear age. Apocalyptic stresses that human beings must choose sides, for or against God, but it is God himself who decides when the final battle will be fought; and ultimately it is God, the divine warrior, who fights and controls the outcome of the battle. God's human allies are necessarily subordinate, although participating fully, in this process. The omnipotent Bomb, on the other hand, is itself powerless until human beings use it. This situation is complicated by the human sense of powerlessness and the very real ways in which humans have abdicated their control and put the Bomb in control. But among our perceptions of nuclear weapons there is always at least some component of awareness that the Bomb is a human invention that is deployed and implemented by human decision. This dimension of human control in the nuclear situation puts us, quite simply, in the place that had formerly been reserved for God.

In discussing the Bomb as symbol of omnipotence, we noted the dilemma that Bomb-possessors must endure: having found ourselves now omnipotent gods, we are deeply ambivalent toward our own infinitude. And we suggested that the Bomb's own annihilating power may attract us as the ultimate solution to this problem. How much more attractive it is when this solution appears as the inevitable culmination of, and final escape from, history and all its ills.

Such a vision of the meaning of nuclear war must, of course, affect one's vision of the symbolic meaning of nuclear weapons today, before any war is fought. It is inevitable that those who share this vision—and it is hard to escape its influence completely—will have their perception of the Bomb tinged, and perhaps pervaded, by that feeling of heroic victory that has enticed virtually all humans in some way or another. The Bomb has tremendously increased the intensity of power involved in war, and it has made all of us warriors who wield that power, especially when governments encourage us to identify our personal power with our nation's power. Thus the appeal of being heroic warriors has been tremendously increased as well. It is hard to resist the temptation to be St. George, knowing that one is destined to kill the dragon, survive, and feel the joy of rebirth, especially when it seems so easy to do— just push the button.

Science fiction and apocalyptic imagination provide powerful images that shape our response to the possibility of nuclear war by offering vivid representations of the myth of heroic survival. One might argue, of course, that we know that these are "just fictions" and that, while they might reflect our wishes and fantasies, when it comes to actual preparation for nuclear war we are more hard-headed and realistic. For some individuals this may be true. But as a society, our "real" attitude is also highly charged with this myth. Since the beginning of the nuclear age, the government has officially supported and propagated a version of the survival myth that might be called "the myth of civil defense." Again, it is important to stress that "myth" does not mean "lie." If any story about the experience of unlimited power may be said to constitute a myth, then the government's projection of a "scenario" for nuclear war is a myth, whether it corresponds to the actuality of such a war perfectly or not at all. While the various agencies of the government work with a wide variety of scenarios, the scenario that is officially presented to the public at large is that of the civil-defense agencies (whose official names change frequently but whose viewpoint remains essentially the same).

The basic attitude, as reflected in the Defense Civil Preparedness Agency's 1977 pamphlet "Protection in the Nuclear Age," is that nuclear war would be, for most Americans, a temporary inconvenience of perhaps two weeks' duration, after which the Enemy would be defeated and life would be better than ever. The pamphlet begins by conceding that "undoubtedly, millions of Americans would die if a nuclear attack should occur." "However," it immediately adds, "studies show that tens of millions would survive the initial effects of blast and heat. Many more would survive these initial effects if they had blast and heat-resistant shelters, or if they could relocate to less vulnerable areas before an attack."[1] The impression created here is that even without use of shelters, the ratio of survivors to fatalities would be 10 to 1. A few pages later, the pamphlet is apparently even more encouraging: the tens of millions, the 90 percent who survive, would be outside the zone of serious injury as well as death.[2]

They would still face the danger of fallout, but this danger can apparently be survived quite easily with some elementary precautions:

People can protect themselves against fallout radiation, and have a good chance of surviving it, by staying inside a fallout shelter. In most cases, the fallout radiation level outside the shelter would decrease rapidly enough to permit people to leave the shelter within a few days. Even in communities that receive heavy accumulations of fallout particles, people soon might be able to leave shelter for a few minutes or a few hours at a time in order to perform emergency tasks. In most places, it is unlikely that full-time shelter occupancy would be required for more than a week or two.[3]

This myth of survival appeals consistently to the magical prestige of government scientific studies, and on this basis offers assurance that there would be little disruption of ordinary life: "From many studies, the Federal Government has determined that enough food and water would be available after an attack to sustain our surviving citizens. However, temporary food shortages might occur in some areas, until food was shipped there from other areas. . . . the danger of people receiving harmful doses of fallout radiation through food, water, or milk is very small."[4] Fallout is not much of a problem because it occurs, according to the pamphlet, in large particles that can easily be brushed or swept away.[5]

It is essential, however, to have a shelter, and the bulk of the pamphlet is concerned with instructions for building and living in a shelter. Shelters are not hard to build; they can even double as basement snack bars or backyard toolsheds.[6] Living in a fallout shelter is rather inconvenient, but manageable if one follows a few simple rules, especially since even part-time shelter life need last only a week or two.[7] In fact, the instructions for preparing for shelter life are quite similar to popular how-to-do-it books for family camping outings. If one is fortunate enough to be in a public shelter, "you probably would not need to know a great deal about managing food, water, and sanitation. A shelter manager and his assistants would handle these problems with the cooperation of all in the shelter."[8] The role of the fallout shelter here is strikingly similar to the huts that are built for initiates in puberty rites of many traditional cultures. The initiates are totally under the direction of masters who guide them through their symbolic death, assuring them that if they follow directions their rebirth into the spiritual status of adulthood is assured.

The rebirth following nuclear war is assured because "if an enemy should threaten to attack the United States, you would not be alone. The entire Nation would be mobilizing to repulse the attack, destroy the enemy, and hold down our own loss of life. Much assistance would be available to you."[9] Such reassurance encourages us to identify ourselves with the Nation (note the capital letter), which will inevitably repulse the attack and destroy the Enemy. Thus it encourages us to picture ourselves in the role of warrior, playing the lead in the apocalyptic drama. It also implies that we need not even question whether the Nation will continue its normal life, supporting us in the style to which we are accustomed. This impression is reinforced by the assertion that key workers in vital industries and services would continue working throughout the war period. (Apparently it is these workers who would ship food to us in case of shortages.)

The pamphlet also offers us another vision of heroic survival—relocation. In this myth, rather than taking shelter in our home-towns, those of us in target areas (all urban areas with more than 50,000 population) would flee temporarily to more remote locations where the populace would be waiting with open arms to assure our common survival.[10] This whole process would be well organized and orderly. Here we recognize the ancient mythological motif of the flight to the wilderness, the escape from the snares of civilization, which is a widespread variant of the myth of spiritual rebirth. In this myth the hero experiences the emptiness, the stillness, the organic naturalness of the wilderness, and he finds spiritual refreshment by absorbing these qualities, so that he can return to civilization with a renewed being. Most of us, in case of nuclear war with a long advance warning, would be able to share in this experience, according to this pamphlet. But those of us designated as key workers would have either to remain in our cities at our jobs or else commute to our jobs from the relocation centers.[11] The implication here, as elsewhere, is that life goes on more or less as usual despite the temporary disruption and inconvenience.

Thus, when the one- or two-week disruption ends, the world will be essentially unchanged—except, of course, for the central fact that we shall have experienced the most immense release of destructive power in the history of the world. We shall have lived through the most awesome initiatory terrors imaginable. The pamphlet gives little attention to this annihilation. It provides a complex chart, with quite small print, describing the destructive effects of nuclear blasts, and it does mention the millions of deaths and the ensuing dangers from fallout. But, as we have seen, it hastily skips over these to assure us at length of the likelihood that we shall survive with little permanent harm if we take a few precautionary measures. And it mentions absolutely nothing about our psychological or emotional condition, our need to cope with unprecedented terror. The civil-defense agencies offer us an easy rebirth with only the slightest tinge of initiatory death. Perhaps this is best symbolized by a sketch in the pamphlet illustrating the proper procedure for someone caught out in the open with no possible shelter when a nuclear bomb explodes: it shows a man lying in a fetal position, with hands over head. The text reads, "If no cover is available, simply lie down on the ground and curl up."[12] And, we might add, await your rebirth.

To some, this pamphlet might seem like good sensible advice. To some it will seem the ultimate in monstrous black humor. Many will find their opinion somewhere between these extremes. But it is clear that the sponsors of such a pamphlet have a very clear message to convey to the public. Whether that message turns out to be totally consonant or totally dissonant with the reality of a nuclear war, it is definitely consonant with the myth of heroic survival that we have been discussing here. It gives the government's stamp of legitimacy to the basic structure of that myth, and thus indirectly to other variants of the myth, such as those found in science fiction and apocalyptic.

Of course, there are good reasons to believe that the government's scenario will turn out to be largely irrelevant in an actual war. The government itself, through the Congress, has published studies of the effects of nuclear war that make the civil-defense precautions seem highly ineffectual. These government studies, moreover, deal at length with the situation after the two-week shelter period, and their findings are uniformly dismal. Ironically, it is the executive branch of government, through the president and other high officials, that has best summarized the skepticism about the civil-defense view. Many of these leaders, in numerous administrations, have said flatly that nuclear war between the superpowers would be mutual suicide. This opinion obviously contradicts the government's official advice to its citizens. Moreover, the pamphlet itself is hardly internally consistent (although its overall theme is carried through from beginning to end), and it is often vague to the point of bewilderment. Its general tone is that things will probably be okay—although we're not quite sure of the details—so there's really nothing to worry about. It seems likely that the authors were inspired much more by myth and hopes than by careful study.

This is hardly surprising, since the myth, beyond its specific political usefulness for specific political interests, has always been much more appealing than a chaotic, unpredictable, ungraspable reality. Myth gives form to immense power, making it possible for our limited minds to relate to the experience of power as a meaningful event. And few myths have been as appealing and enduring as the myth of heroic survival and rebirth. Its fascination reaches to the very highest levels of political leadership: in 1981 the Defense Department's ranking official for research on nuclear war advocated "digging holes" as an effective defense against nuclear attack. When the alert sounds, he advised, everyone should dig a hole two or three feet deep, crawl in, then cover it somehow, and wait. This initiatory burial could be counted on to secure a postwar rebirth: "If there are enough shovels to go around, everybody's going to make it. . . . It's the dirt that does it."[13] A more classical form of the myth found its way to the Senate floor when Senator Richard Russell rose to advocate more nuclear weapons with a resounding affirmation: "If we have to start over with another Adam and Eve, I want them to be Americans."[14]

8

SACRIFICE AND
MARTYRDOM

The myths of death and rebirth have been acted out countless times in countless ways. Perhaps the most frequent and widespread of these reenactments, however, have been through the ritual of sacrifice. "Sacrifice" may be defined very broadly as a destruction that is believed to yield beneficial results. Nuclear weapons are, in everyone's opinion, immensely destructive; their proponents find potential benefits in them; these benefits are closely linked with the theme of death and rebirth; hence it seems plausible that the concept of sacrifice might help us to understand the symbolic meaning of nuclear weapons.

There are many interpretations of sacrifice and its role in human life, and it seems likely that no one interpretation can be valid for all sacrifices. Perhaps the most common view is that sacrifice is a gift to a god. One might easily interpret the money spent on nuclear armament, and the lives and property destroyed in a nuclear blast, as gifts to the unlimited power embodied in the Bomb. But why do the gods desire gifts at all? Again various interpretations have been advanced. In some cases the motivation centers on the principle of *do ut des*—"I give so that you may give." Here there is often the belief that the god, having given us life and material prosperity, has depleted its own potency and needs to be energized. The creation of life in our world entails a reduction of the life-force in the divine realm, as it were, and so to augment the divine realm we must reduce—that is, destroy—life in our realm. Thus, while money and property are sometimes offered as sacrifices, in the vast majority of cases a living being must be the victim. For only by actually destroying life can we act out the basic principle involved here, acknowledging that the god who gives life must also consume and reclaim it.

Perhaps a similar awareness led Robert Oppenheimer, the "father of the atomic bomb," to remember a passage from the Bhagavad-Gita as he watched the first atomic explosion: "I am become Death, shatterer of worlds."[1] Oppenheimer knew the Gita well, and so he understood that the god Krishna, who utters these words, also declares himself to be the source and giver of all life. Yet, because all life is ephemeral, all must return to him; he is "death that snatches all," "devouring all worlds."[2] So Krishna urges his disciple Arjuna to acknowledge this cosmic fact by making all his life a sacrifice to the god, since all must be given back eventually anyway. It is striking, though, that Krishna's true nature as devourer is not apparent until he reveals his true unlimited form to Arjuna, displaying his infinite power completely. In a sense the atom was always both the origin and the shatterer of all worlds, but only in manifesting its unlimited power in 1945 did that reality become apparent. Perhaps Oppenheimer was consciously aware of what many others realize only unconsciously—that a nuclear war might be seen as giving back to the god that which had come from it and always belonged to it.

Gifts to the gods mean much more, though, than merely recirculating cosmic energy. Those who offer the sacrifice frequently hope to experience the power that is released and retain at least some of it directly for themselves. Among the Dogon of Africa, for example, life is held to depend on a sufficient amount of the abstract sacred power called *nyama*: "One of the functions of sacrifice is that the current established by the effluxion of the victim's blood, and the release of *nyama* which accompanies it, can alleviate the lack which the person sacrificed for is suffering from, and so help him to make good the loss of substance which he has undergone."[3] Similarly, the sacrifices that Krishna asks for in the Gita are intended ultimately to release the abstract sacred power, *brahman*, within the sacrificer and thereby transform his life.

Oppenheimer's reference to Krishna was particularly apt in this regard, too, for Krishna is at once both a personal deity (as are most recipients of sacrifice) and the embodiment of an impersonal cosmic force. Krishna therefore reflects the transcendence of the distinction between personal and impersonal images of the divine. In a somewhat similar way, our perceptions of nuclear weapons incorporate both sides of this dichotomy as well. The power of the atom is, for us, much like *nyama* or *brahman*—abstract, impersonal, cosmic, and unlimited in scope. But when we speak of "the Bomb" or "the big one," there are overtones of an almost personal reality. And the only two nuclear weapons ever used in wartime had quite personal names: the first "Little Boy," the second "Fat Man" (after Winston Churchill). We have seen how popular imagination may be drawn to the image of the *big whoosh*, which engulfs its victims and returns them back to the formless state of pure energy from which they originated. Whether the source of this *whoosh* be viewed as personal or impersonal may not make much difference; as with the divinity of the Bhagavad-Gita, the two approaches are complementary. In either case, the *big whoosh* can easily be seen as a sacrifice to the Bomb that releases infinite power—power latent in both the victims and the recipient—and fills us, the offerers of the sacrifice, with that cosmic power that has hitherto been absent in our lives.

It may seem paradoxical, of course, that those who offer up the nuclear sacrifice, hoping to benefit from it, are also its victims. But the logic of sacrifice resolves this paradox with little trouble. For in many sacrifices (and perhaps implicitly in all) the victim is a symbol or substitute for the donor. Ultimately those who offer sacrifice want to offer themselves to the god. The giving of a gift always implies a closer relationship between giver and receiver. As the desire for relationship increases, it tends inevitably to culminate in a desire for complete union. But the desire to go on living is stronger than the desire to be consumed in the god, and so some substitute is found that will represent the very being of the giver. This is another reason why living victims are so preponderant. If the givers ultimately want to give themselves, at least symbolically, they approach this goal more closely when they give a living thing of great value.

Sacrifice often appears wasteful or self-destructive to the outsider; but it is precisely the great value of the victim to the giver that makes the victim able to function as a vicarious representation of the giver's own life. If the Bomb is our prime symbol of limitless power, security, and other highly valued realities, it is natural that we shall want to enter into as close a relationship as possible with it. Only in such an intimate relationship can we hope to absorb these realities into our own lives. To do so perfectly, we would have to die as sacrificial victims; perhaps we are prepared to do so in the near future. For the present, we offer immense amounts of that which we value most—our money—as sacrificial substitutes.

The power that is released in sacrifice fills both the offerer and the recipient, but is actually released from the victim. Hence the victim itself can come to be seen as filled with power and sacralized through the ritual. Perhaps the most famous example of this is the "totem," the animal that is said among some peoples to embody the sacrality inherent in both the clan or tribe and its gods. In some sacrifices, the victim is eaten by the sacrificers, apparently in a symbolic meal that is shared with the god. Here we find both the attempt to evoke closer relationship, since eating meals together always has this effect, and the attempt to create a sort of "power field" shared in common by people, victims, and gods. Gaston Bouthoul has suggested that "war has all the characteristics of a feast, whose principal function, according to [Emile] Durkheim, is to unify the group."[4] Because the feast also involves large expenditures of resources, including sacrifices, and the modification of some moral rules, and produces a sense of collective exaltation, "as every one of these characteristics is found in war, war might be regarded as the supreme feast."[5] This would be even more true of the unprecedented scale of a nuclear war.

In war, of course, the Enemy functions as the victim, and it often appears that the conqueror wants to devour the Enemy as the sacrificers devour the victim. Yet the ideology of war, especially in apocalyptic contexts, often involves dedicating the victims to the god for whom one fights. If the ideology prevents the conqueror from making any use of the spoils of war, as in the biblical book of Joshua, the Enemy becomes a victim given wholly as a gift to the god. But if, as in modern warfare, this idea of "fighting for God" is tempered with a desire for more material advantages, the situation resembles the sacrifice in which gods and sacrificers share together in being nourished by the sacrifice. The sacrificial meal also functions to bring the members of the community closer together, as does the common effort expended in war. The comradeship of war can itself generate intense experiences of power, as Gray points out: "We feel earnest and gay at such moments because we are liberated from our individual impotence and are drunk with the power that union with our fellows brings."[6] Yet this sense of power is immeasurably heightened by the conviction that one is sharing fellowship with a god as well, for it is divinity that is the symbol of ultimate power.

To see the Enemy as a victim shared with, or consumed by, a god, however, one must symbolically transfer the Enemy into the realm of sacrality even before destroying it. This is one of the meanings involved in seeing the Enemy as "the devil," for the devil, while in one sense the opposite of a god, is in one sense a sacred being too: it is outside the realm of the ordinary, the profane. There are in fact interesting mythological traditions that speak of the close unity, even the brotherhood, of gods and devils. Thus to see the Enemy as a devil-figure is to make the conquest of the Enemy basically a means of absorbing the sacred power that it embodies. In such a war, some of one's own property and even life is inevitably destroyed too. But this becomes acceptable not only because it is seen as a gift to god, but also because that which is destroyed becomes, like the Enemy, sacred. Thus its destruction is a means of releasing sacred power that is ultimately absorbed by the victor and used in the process of rebuilding and renewal.

Sacrifice differs from war, however, because the victim is, from the outset, under the community's control. The amount of death and loss to be incurred is not at all a matter of chance, as it is in war. In fact some interpreters of sacrifice lay greatest stress on this aspect: the process of death and rebirth is acknowledged as necessary, but it is given a strict shape and structure. Thus sacrifice comes to offer a sense of control over the process of life and death. Ritualized death may be used to forestall or avert natural death, as in cases where famine, flood, or other natural disasters are said to be alleviated by sacrifice. It may also be seen as releasing a sacred power that cleanses the environment of evil or impurity. Christian apocalypticism, with its image of "the lamb of God who takes away the sins of the world," reflects this aspect of sacrifice. In such situations, and others as well, sacrifice may be called a ritual of defense. In sacrifice, "the common aim is to defend the donors . . . [against] the inescapable vulnerability of humanity, vulnerability to the unexpected, unpredictable and uncontrollable fact of disease or hunger or war . . . and ultimately of course to the totally inescapable vulnerability to death and annihilation."[7]

While some sacrifices display this meaning more clearly than others, it may very well be implicit in all. (Perhaps it is appropriate that the agency that calls on us to make sacrifice in facing the Enemy is called the Defense Department.) But the crucial point is that through sacrifice not only do we express our sense of vulnerability but, more importantly, we believe that we have overcome that vulnerability and averted its threat. Ultimately, then, sacrifice, the symbolic destruction of our life, may be a means to convince ourselves that our lives need never be destroyed. By establishing a sufficiently strong relationship with limitless power, we feel that we have ensured our security and freed ourselves from the threat of annihilation; we have gained some form of immortality. Yet all of this demands that we shed blood that is, at least symbolically, our own.

The sense of control over the environment that modern technology provides may seem to make such sacrifices for defense irrelevant. But a modern anthropologist, discussing sacrifice in this light, adds a note that is of particular interest in the present discussion: "We may think ourselves exempt from this, but enormously as the threshold of vulnerability has been raised by advances in science, technology, medicine, and social organization, the sense of vulnerability still remains with us—in matters of health, economic and social well being, personal and collective existence, etc. Does it not lie behind the whole range of compensating values and practices reflected in our political ideologies and in our moral norms? Does it not play a large part in the proliferation of escapist and salvationist cults?"[8] And, we may ask, does it not contribute significantly to our ambivalent embrace of the Bomb?

Beyond the fundamental religious meanings of sacrifice, there are also some relevant ways in which sacrifice affects the sociological life of a community. The ability to destroy is itself a form of power that lends status and prestige to the one who displays it. This appears in the well-known ritual of the potlatch, in which members of the Kwakiutl tribe would give away and waste huge amounts of property, and sometimes life, to demonstrate their ability to do so and consequently their high social standing. In some cases, two members of the tribe would compete in destruction, each seeing his rival's potlatch as a challenge to his own prestige and thus feeling compelled to outdo the rival. It has been suggested that the nuclear arms race may be seen as a modern form of potlatch, "a cycle of prodigality-challenge in which each of the adversaries, by wasting an enormous amount of wealth on armaments, hopes to intimidate the other and prove his own superiority."[9]

This suggestion leads us to repeat an important observation: all the aspects of sacrifice we have been reviewing here are relevant not only to the willingness to destroy in war, but also to the even more avid willingness to offer huge peacetime resources to the Bomb through ever-increasing expenditures for armaments. Another important social function of sacrifice should be mentioned in this regard. In many cultures, certain kinds of sacrifice may be offered only by the king, chief, or other political authority. In such cases, the power to destroy is a symbolic expression of the leader's power to dispense over all existence. Thus the government may be led to symbolize and thereby reinforce its power by demanding ever-increasing sacrifices from the people. When billions of dollars are spent to increase the government's capacity to annihilate at will, it surely deserves to be seen as such a form of sacrifice.

Every act of destruction is in some sense a breach of the existing order and so generates new power, as the transition from structure to chaos always does. But on some occasions ritualized acts of illegal or antisocial destruction may be carried out intentionally to imbue the actors with sacred power. The greater the level of destruction, and the more contrary it is to societal norms, the greater the power. Perhaps the physical power of nuclear weapons themselves is augmented by the power that comes from knowing that they may be used to violate the most elementary principles of morality on which human order depends.

A recent theory of sacrifice suggests further dimensions of this aspect of the subject. René Girard has argued that sacrifice is primarily a way for members of a community to discharge the violence that they feel for one another in a socially harmless way. The inevitable stresses and tensions of life in society, he claims, lead each of us to desire to commit antisocial acts of violence against our fellows. But if we all get together and choose a common victim—or a common enemy—we can discharge our violence and simultaneously reaffirm our bonds and commitments to live peaceably with each other. While Girard's claim to have discovered *the* single meaning of all sacrifice is probably exaggerated, there is certainly an element of this in every sacrifice, and it appears quite clearly in the relative harmony that reigns within most nations at war.

A related approach to sacrifice is offered by Victor Turner who puts great stress on the usefulness of periods of "anti-structure" or release from the burden of the social order. It seems quite plausible that the absence of such legitimate experiences of "anti-structure" builds up pressure in our own society, making the desire for some sort of sacrificial act even more intense. But even in traditional societies the pressures of structure can engender conflicts that need to be resolved if the society is to survive. The survival mechanism often turns out to be some form of ritualized or stylized drama in which the whole process of crisis and resolution is acted out, ending in a restored feeling of cooperation and well-being.

Sacrifice often forms the climax of this drama, and it is easy to see how a sacrifice can in itself embody the entire drama of conflict, destruction, resolution, and renewal. Yet in all of this the participants are conscious of playing their assigned and stylized roles as actors in the drama. The dramatic quality of the nuclear arms race, with its language of "scenarios" and "theaters of war," may be seen as a striking analogue to this process, once we realize that the arms race and the contemplated use of those arms may be contemporary forms of sacrifice. Certainly the intensity of the drama and the willingness to think seriously about the ultimate sacrifice do increase in times of social as well as political crisis.

All in all, there seems to be ample evidence that the dynamics of sacrifice play an important role in the symbolic meanings of nuclear weapons. But the obviously crucial point has yet to be stated: the use of nuclear weapons demands not only a willingness to sacrifice one's property and social structure and values—the symbolic substitutes for life—but a willingness to sacrifice quite literally one's own life and the lives of one's loved ones. We are talking about real human sacrifice, and the stakes are thus infinitely higher. Yet human sacrifice is well known in the history of human culture. There are many examples, of course, of sacrificing the enemy or the stranger. These are largely comprehensible in terms of the discussion offered thus far. But a few specific points ought to be noted.

If every sacrifice is in one sense a substitute for one's own life, another human being is the ultimately desirable choice. Generally one does not want to sacrifice a human being whom one values (although we shall note exceptions to this), and so an enemy or a stranger is a prime candidate. We have already seen how the enemy may become sacralized as a representation of the devil; the stranger, too, is often seen as the embodiment of extraordinary and thus sacred power. To kill either is to release the power inherent in them. Yet in the modern world, where we frequently know few of our neighbors and bureaucracy forces anonymity upon us, the members of our own community are often just as much strangers as those living on the other side of the world. As we contemplate those who might die in a nuclear war, our unwillingness and inability to conceive of our own deaths is easily extended to the few people who really matter in our lives. The large faceless mass of others, even though they be nominally our fellow citizens, are in fact strangers whose lives may easily seem expendable.

The modern world has shown many instances of nations willingly sacrificing large segments of their own population that were considered expendable. Although these "expendable people" are often marked off by some minority status of race, religion, class or the like, it is not a large step from this attitude to considering all strangers as expendable. This step becomes even easier when "defense-intellectuals" reduce one's fellow citizens to numbers in a computer. There is also a temptation to blame one's own difficulties in life on "them," the strangers, and perhaps to see the Bomb as a means of ridding the world of "them." It has been suggested that the prime function of war is to rid one's own nation of excess population, and Richard Garwin's warning is relevant here: if the faith that the world is getting better "were largely replaced by a belief that the world would be a better place with a lot fewer people (even a lot fewer Americans or Soviets), a major barrier to nuclear war would be removed."[10]

Yet at some point everyone must become aware that it is not only the enemy and the stranger who will die in a nuclear war; there is every likelihood that many people whom one loves will also be sacrificed to the Bomb. This consideration has not prevented nations from preparing for nuclear war, any more than similar considerations prevented earlier nations from preparing for and fighting conventional wars. In fact, psychoanalysis has taken the theory of war as population control one step further and seen in it a deliberate attempt by parents to subject their sons to the risk of death. In the Freudian view, all parents unconsciously desire the deaths of their children. Since war is an acted-out expression of a universal and inescapable fantasy, every parent unconsciously wants war, and so war is understandably universal.

It is a striking fact that, in all the Western religions, the man who serves as the model of spiritual perfection—Abraham—earns the right to become the ideal by his willingness to kill his only son. Even more striking is Christianity's God, who goes one step further than Abraham and actually allows his only son to die. The meaning of these motifs is, of course, endlessly debated, and the Freudian interpretation is only one of many. The traditions themselves assert that these are "one-time-only" extraordinary events, which are not to be imitated literally. Nevertheless they are paradigms for a wide variety of recommended acts of spiritual self-denial and sacrifice, and they stand as the ultimate examples of praiseworthy behavior, despite the fact that they speak of morally reprehensible deeds. Moreover, these unique events are held to initiate that sacred history which will find its consummation in the apocalypse. When apocalyptic thinking becomes more prominent, as it has in the nuclear age, so do these models. The theme of "As it was in the beginning, so shall it be in the end" is pervasive in all religions; perhaps it has a special importance in this context.

The jarring clash between ethics and spirituality here prompted Søren Kierkegaard to meditate at length on the meaning of Abraham's action, in an essay (*Fear and Trembling*) that laid some of the basic foundations for twentieth-century thought. Kierkegaard might well have had a prophetic premonition of the nuclear age when he brought the category of "the absurd" into a central place here. He suggested that Abraham could break the ethical norm because of his extraordinary spiritual status; he was a "knight of faith," which means that he believed that he could sacrifice his son and still somehow get him back, even though he knew this was absurd. In fact he believed precisely because it was absurd, as Tertullian claimed a Christian must do. Yet Kierkegaard warned how easily any father might deceive himself into thinking that he, too, had the right to kill his son and thereby win spiritual glory. Only those who sincerely believed in the absurd, to the depths of their whole being, might contemplate such a deed, warned Kierkegaard.

In the nuclear age, Kierkegaard's thoughts take on a strange new significance. We have seen the deep confusion in popular thinking on these subjects; while there is surely recognition of the absurdity of nuclear war, there is also the deep-seated belief in heroic survival, despite its absurdity. Is it possible that the modern world is increasingly filled with Kierkegaard's would-be imitators of Abraham? Indeed most people who accept nuclear armament act as if they believed despite the absurdity, perhaps even because of the absurdity. But this belief occurs among a population that is increasingly psychically numb and therefore incapable of the kind of deep consideration and understanding that Kierkegaard's Abraham displayed. The plethora of contradiction and ambiguity that plagues us today seems to make it impossible for one to be a true "knight of faith." For the "knight of faith" must know with absolute certainty the meaning of what he does and the reason for which he does it; he must be spiritually dedicated to a single idea with no ambivalence at all (an ideal that Kierkegaard thought practically impossible to attain). Thus we may well be attracted to an imitation of Abraham's sacrifice, as Kierkegaard suggests, and yet be committing the most abominable of immoralities—the sacrifice of our children.

From the sacrifice of strangers and enemies to that of loved ones, there is a line that leads inexorably to the final inescapable conclusion: in a nuclear war, we would each have to be prepared to lose our own lives as well. To understand nuclear weapons, we must therefore look at self-sacrifice—the willingness of human beings to give up their own lives in the belief that such a sacrifice will somehow produce beneficial results. In many cases, of course, there is a belief that the martyr will be rewarded with some sort of paradisal afterlife; both Christianity and Islam, particularly in their earlier stages, were heavily influenced by such a belief. Today there are still many who hold fast to such a belief, which may be very potent when combined with an apocalyptic view of history. The result is a conviction that a heavenly reward awaits all those who die in the final battle to purge the world of evil, while those who withhold the ultimate sacrifice prove by their reluctance that they are really on the side of evil and thus are doomed to the torments of hell.

The willingness to martyr oneself certainly does not depend on belief in a personal afterlife. In modern warfare, many are led to give up their lives voluntarily because they believe that some value higher than personal life can thereby be attained or defended. Often in combat it is the survival of one's immediate group that is the goal; by identifying oneself with the group completely, self-sacrifice becomes a means to immortality; "I may fall, but I do not die, for that which is real in me goes forward and lives on in the comrades for whom I gave up my life."[11] There is also, of course, self-sacrifice to preserve the values for which the group stands and the ideologies that bind the group together, and death in the service of these also creates a kind of immortality, as the "best part" of one lives on in the survival of the eternal values for which one has died. If these values are religious, self-sacrifice takes on the functions of all forms of sacrifice; the victim enters into permanent communion with sacred power and in fact becomes sacralized.

Thus the likelihood that a given individual will die in a nuclear war need not necessarily deter that individual from supporting preparation for such a war and willingness to fight it. Insofar as individuals accept the myth of heroic survival, they need not necessarily picture themselves as physical survivors. It is enough to feel assured, as the apocalyptic believer is assured, that "our side" will inevitably win and endure forever. Yet even if the myth of survival is rejected, there is still a significance and appeal to self-sacrifice in nuclear war. One is, in fact, giving oneself to the repository of limitless power, the symbol of order and eternity, in a very real way. Whereas the giver of a typical sacrifice is consumed by the sacred power in only a symbolic way, the martyr is consumed by and merges with that power quite literally. Even if no rebirth is expected or hoped for, permanent union with limitless power, release from one's impotence and limited structure into a reality of cosmic scale, and forsaking time for absorption in eternity can all be persuasive motivations for contemplating the self-sacrifice of martyrdom. As we have seen, the objection that there is immense self-deception in such an aspiration is hardly likely to weaken its appeal.

Not all who sacrifice themselves in a religious cause do so gladly or eagerly. But there have been martyrs in the history of religion who did actively seek and provoke their own deaths. Early Christianity, with its apocalyptic fervor, offers many examples. When death is a desired and self-inflicted end, it is a form of suicide. So, having traced the ambiguous relationships of life and death through the myth of heroic rebirth, the apocalyptic vision, and the ritual of sacrifice and martyrdom, we must now turn to the ultimate existential question—suicide.

9

MUTUAL SUICIDE

When we think about nuclear war between the superpowers, one of the first phrases to come to mind is inevitably "mutual suicide." This concept is the basis for the theory of MAD, a prime justification for nuclear armament, and for much of the sentiment for nuclear disarmament. We have already seen that the government itself, through its civil-defense agencies, seems less than convinced of its validity. Nevertheless, government leaders, and many other people, continue to repeat it frequently enough that it bears careful examination. Again, we are not interested in the empirical accuracy of this prediction; whether in fact a nation could survive an all-out nuclear war remains, for some, a very grave but still debatable question. But there is no doubt that "mutual suicide" is one of the most powerful images of nuclear war at work in everyone's mind, and thus it is certain that the symbolic meaning of the Bomb is somehow related to the issue of suicide. In fact, a survey of some leading contemporary theorizing about suicide shows many striking points of contact with our discussion of the symbolic dimensions of nuclear weapons.

The theory of MAD depends on the assumption that national leaders, being rational people, would not begin a war that means suicide for their nation. We have seen that there is ample reason to question that assumption, as well as the prior assumption that national leaders are always rational. Furthermore we have just noted that even supposedly rational people have been willing to engage in various forms of human sacrifice. Now we must add that

the assumption that only madmen contemplate suicide is also
highly questionable. Stengel states: "It is reasonable not to accept
the suicidal act alone as a criterion of mental disorder. . . . On the
average one third of the people who commit suicide have been
suffering from a neurosis or psychosis or a severe personality
disorder."[1]

Those who attempt or contemplate suicide often hold logically
contradictory thoughts about it, and thus they are irrational, but
this does not make them mad in the psychiatric sense. The
contradictions are, rather, reflections of an ambivalence that may,
at some level, be present in all of us. Most suicides "do not want
either to live or to die, but to do both at the same time—usually one
more than the other."[2] Ambivalence over suicide is even apparent
in the teachings of the Christian church, which officially bans
suicide and yet recognizes its appeal by praising martyrdom. The
ambivalence surrounding suicide, religious and otherwise, suggests
that the suicide is not actually sure whether, through such an act,
life will be extinguished or renewed: "Suicide, then, is a highly
ambivalent action. Even those individuals with very serious intentions of dying by suicide rarely give up hope of living."[3] We shall
explore further dimensions of this ambivalence and hope directly.
At this point, however, it should be apparent that national leaders
who affirm the MAD-ness of nuclear war as "mutual suicide" and
yet simultaneously prepare for a postwar future, talking of a serious
commitment to use the weapons, are behaving very much like those
individuals who contemplate or attempt taking their own lives.

Certain characteristics do seem to occur in the mental states of
most if not all potential suicides. One of these is a sense of
hopelessness, which many think is the primary factor in bringing on
attempts at suicide. This, in turn, is linked to a feeling of powerlessness, inability to change one's situation for the better: "Present
is an overwhelming sense of being hemmed in, blocked, thwarted,
a sense of the impossibility of achieving form or meaning. . . .
Killing oneself may appear to be the only way to break out of the
'trap.' "[4] Such a feeling of hopelessness and powerlessness is often
cited as an element of that meaninglessness which many see as
pervasive in the present age. We have noted how the Bomb
reinforces such a feeling, and now it appears that this feeling may

in turn lead to a willingness to contemplate using the Bomb, even when such use is seen as suicidal.

This feeling also deeply affects the attitude toward the future: "One's ultimate involvements are so impaired that one is simply unable to imagine a psychologically livable future."[5] In some cases, "the self-inflicted deaths relate primarily to the individual's falling out of his sense of a procession of generations. . . . The person who falls out of his society or out of his lineage is a person who has lost investment in his own 'post-self'—that which continues after his death."[6] Because the Bomb makes the possibility of any future questionable, heightening the tendency to "live for the moment," it must also heighten this aspect of the suicidal feeling. The feeling of losing continuity deepens the suicidal trap even further by intensifying psychic numbing, the feeling that one is already in some sense dead, for "one must see one's self as already dead in order to kill it."[7] "Death in life" heightens the ambivalence of not knowing whether one wants to be dead or alive and leads to an apathy of not caring whether one lives or dies. Such a person often "has taken as many of the world's assaults as he cares to take; his limits or tolerance for continuing his bargain with life have been reached."[8]

Again, many contemporary thinkers would see this as a characterization of much of modern society as a whole. One philosopher suggests: "Contemporary man shows distinct signs of having lost the animal *joie de vivre*—the exultation of simply being alive. One could even assert that many—and this includes numbers of those who enjoy physical and social well-being—do not really care whether they are alive or dead."[9] Thus it may be necessary to see many aspects of modern culture as "partial suicides"—behaviors that reflect ambivalence about life, yet a simultaneous fear to actually kill oneself—"such as certain patterns of psychosis, addiction, alcoholism, prostitution, delinquency, incivility, underachievement, and ennui. There are numerous ways of committing partial suicide and permitting partial death, all truncations of the spirit."[10] Lifton has argued at length that many behaviors and patterns in our culture reflect this sense of "partial death" or "death in life," and that all of these are in some way linked to the mass deaths of the present century, which are symbolized by the Bomb. Thus the psychic numbing generated and embodied in nuclear weapons enhances the urge toward suicide and thus the urge to use these weapons. Moreover, Lifton claims that suicide is much more likely if one already has experienced some model for it, which he calls "death equivalents."[11] There seems, then, to be a vicious circle in which nuclear weapons as "death equivalents" produce, in a variety of ways, the states of mind and feeling that make suicide more likely, and these states in turn promote more willingness to consider the use of "suicidal" weapons.

A further dimension of this circle lies in the sense of unreality that is common to both suicidal states and perceptions of the Bomb. Many of those who pursue "partial death," or are accident prone, may be pursuing death yet denying the reality of what they are doing.[12] Even those who actually attempt suicide may not face the reality of their actions: "It is remarkable that conscious preoccupation with notions about death is rare before suicidal acts."[13] And we have noted that many who try to kill themselves rarely give up hope of living. "We know from many studies that many suicidal people do not really think that they will be dead when they kill themselves."[14] This is certainly more common in a society in which death itself is often denied and treated as unreal, although it also reflects the apparently congenital inability of humans to imagine their own deaths. We have seen at length how this denial is related as both cause and effect to the unreality that surrounds nuclear weapons.

Paradoxically, though, this sense of unreality may arise not only from the irrationality involved, but also from the peculiarly "rational" logic of suicide. As Alvarez describes this logic, his words might apply equally well to the thinking of defense-intellectuals and government officials on nuclear war: "To the extent to which suicide *is* logical, it is also unreal . . . It is like the unanswerable logic of a nightmare, or like the science-fiction fantasy of being projected suddenly into another dimension: everything makes sense and follows its own strict rules; yet, at the same time, everything is also different, perverted, upside-down"[15] And this world of nightmare logic is one that we must all inhabit, perhaps therefore bringing us all just a bit closer to contemplating the actual deed.

Every act of suicide has many complex and overlapping meanings. Nearly all writers have noted that suicide usually involves, among other things, an attempt to communicate a message to another person through the self-destructive act. Perhaps the most basic message is the cry for help, which may be inherent in every suicide. If nuclear suicide is interpreted in this light, it is hard to see to whom the cry would be directed; perhaps it is to the Bomb itself, the recipient of our sacrifice and symbol of eternal limitless power. Or perhaps the cry, in a moment of deepest despair, is not directed to anyone in particular but is merely a last desperate act in hopes that someone, anyone, will take notice and pity our plight. Another message that may be communicated in suicide is that someone else wants the suicide to die; the suicide "experiences himself as being invited to stop living, and he obliges."[16] If the mass culture of the twentieth century has produced a sense of anonymity and a willingness to sacrifice "expendable people," increasing numbers of us may perceive ourselves as invited by society at large to die, and our willingness to accept the possibility of mass suicide may be a response to that message.

But the most relevant message expressed in many suicides is one of anger and hostility toward another. For nuclear weapons are said by their supporters to be necessary only because we have an enemy who imposes the threat of conflict upon us. If conflict between individuals is a relevant factor in suicide, conflict between nations must surely be relevant in understanding international suicide. Suicide may be seen as a means to punish someone, to get revenge for a real or imagined hurt. This helps to explain Lifton's surprising discovery that some Hiroshima survivors actually wished for a global nuclear war. He cites a woman who put it plainly: "I feel very angry about my unlucky fate. Being angry about it, I sometimes wish that all of the earth would be annihilated."[17] He explains: "The *hibakusha*'s 'underground' wish for ultimate retaliation or total nuclear conflagration can be understood as the most extreme expression of the survivor's embittered world-view . . . which says, in effect: 'I can accept having been singled out for this special degree of suffering only if everybody else is put through it; I can accept the A-bomb only if the world is engulfed in nuclear disaster.' "[18]

If Lifton is correct in claiming that all of us in the nuclear age are touched by the "survivor mentality," then we all may share in some degree the survivor's anger. And the vast majority of us, having no direct experience of suffering through nuclear war, may be all the more easily led to fantasize nuclear suicide as a retaliation against our enemies. Moreover, in our fantasies we may see ourselves escaping the obvious consequences of our actions, while gaining the relief of venting our rage. Alvarez, discussing this dynamic as it appears in many religious dimensions of various cultures, says: "Suicide under these conditions is curiously unreal; it is as though it were committed in the certain belief that the suicide himself would not really die. Instead, he is performing a magical act which will initiate a complex but equally magical ritual ending in the death of his enemy."[19]

The complexity of suicide is compounded, however, by the common observation that those we most hate may be those we most love. Our rage is, therefore, often accompanied by acute feelings of guilt. Freud suggested that suicides might harbor within themselves an objectified other person who was simultaneously the object of love, rage, and guilt feelings. He saw the act of suicide as an attempt to rid the self of the guilt by allowing the objectified other to take its revenge and destroy the guilt by destroying the self. Lifton also found evidence in Hiroshima to support this view, indicating that the anger that led to desire for annihilation was reinforced by extreme guilt feelings. As he summarizes survivors' thinking: "I almost died; I should have died; I did die, or at least I am not really alive; or if I am alive, it is impure of me to be so; anything I do which affirms life is also impure and an insult to the dead, who alone are pure. . . . The survivor feels drawn into permanent union with the force that killed so many others around him"[20] While the result of this is psychic numbing—living as if dead—it can also lead to a desire for actual death; the survivor "becomes overwhelmed by death guilt, experiences a marked diminution of vitality, and embraces a 'death-welcoming' formulation."[21] Again, if all of us see ourselves as survivors and feel guilt toward the innumerable victims of contemporary mass death, we may be propelled by this dynamic toward such a suicidal situation.

Alvarez suggests that the process is even more complex, for the suicides may also cast themselves intentionally (albeit unconsciously) into a powerless role: "The angry child who says, 'I'll die and then you'll be sorry,' is not merely seeking revenge. He is also projecting the guilt and anger that possesses him on those who control his life. In other words, he is defending himself from his own hostility by the mechanism of projective identification; he becomes the victim, they the persecutors."[22] This analysis links the message of revenge to the feeling of powerlessness in the suicide, seeing each as a support for the other. From this point of view, the sense of victimization at the hands of the Enemy (e.g., the claim that "we are behind in the arms race"), the conviction that the Enemy poses a real threat, which must be met with counterthreat and preparations for war, and the desire for revenge and punishment of the Enemy—all appear to be facets of a psychological state that is highly conducive to contemplating suicide.

The feeling of victimization may be compounded by an inability to vent whatever hostility one has at one's enemy. The frustration arising from this inability compounds the anger; the more it builds and remains bottled-up, the more it creates a deep sense of powerlessness and loss of vitality—a primary cause of the suicidal urge. In a world where nations feel unable to vent their hostility upon their enemies because their weaponry is just too lethally dangerous to be used, the same dynamic may be occurring. If it is impossible to express anger without committing suicide, the anger may nevertheless one day burst out, and suicide may seem the most desirable course.

Suicide, however, is not only a reflection of powerlessness. It also may be a fantasized means to escape from that condition. Suicides may be seeking a new form of life, "possessed of unrealistic feelings of omnipotence and omnipresence," in Shneidman's words.[23] In suicide the person who feels helpless asserts at least one final act of free choice and control over life: "For suicide is, after all, the result of a choice," says Alvarez. . . . "Some kind of minimal freedom—the freedom to die in one's own way and in one's own time—has been salvaged from the wreck of all those unwanted necessities."[24] James Hillman notes that there is a direct link between suicide and the affirmation of individuality: "As individuality grows, so does the possibility of suicide. . . . Suicide is the paradigm of our independence from everyone else."[25] Thus a society with relatively loose social constraints, one that places a high premium on individual self-expression, is likely to see an increase in suicide.

Such a tendency toward individualism was one of the features of that Hellenistic culture that we have earlier compared with our contemporary world. We noted that a pervasive feeling of power-lessness at that time led to the worship of Fate and Chance as divinities and to the Stoic indifference that reflects total acceptance of whatever Fate may bring. Yet for the Stoic there was one fundamental means of affirming control over self and escaping the inevitability of Fate: suicide. Seneca wrote: "Foolish man, what do you bemoan, and what do you fear? Wherever you look there is an end of evils. You see that yawning precipice? It leads to liberty. . . . You see that stunted, parched, and sorry tree? From each branch liberty hangs. . . . Do you enquire the road to freedom? You shall find it in every vein of your body."[26] The Stoic might honestly choose suicide as the most rational course, using it to gain power over himself and ultimately over the cosmos.

A feeling of power may in fact be the goal of suicide; killing oneself may come to be seen as the only means to feel potent and alive. The absence of vitality is often a product of fear of death itself; only those who have actually faced death as an inner experience while alive can truly experience life. Hillman writes: "When we refuse the experience of death we also refuse the essential questions of life, and leave life unaccomplished. . . . We are obliged to go to death before it comes to us."[27] Most people do this in a wide variety of symbolic and psychological ways, among which ritual sacrifice was most common in premodern times. But some, like the martyrs, feel compelled to carry the process all the way through to a consciously evoked encounter with actual death. The quest for life and power through killing, a central aspect of our understanding of sacrifice, is also central in this interpretation of suicide: "The impulse to death need not be conceived as an antilife movement; it may be a demand for an encounter with absolute reality, a demand for a fuller life through the death experience. . . . Suicide is the attempt to move from one realm to another by force through death."[28]

When suicide is seen in this light, its connection with the symbolic dimensions of nuclear weapons is obvious. If the Bomb is indeed our fundamental symbol of power, then releasing its power upon ourselves may well be a fantasied means of gaining power and life by passing through death and arising reborn. If we consciously decide to release that power, we gain the added advantage of freedom, for we take control not only over our own lives but over unlimited power as well. And from this sense of control may come a feeling of order that has hitherto been absent. Some suicides approach the act with a hope of gaining clarity and structure: "I had looked for something overwhelming, an experience which would clarify all my confusions."[29] "If I commit suicide, it will not be to destroy myself but to put myself back together again. . . . By suicide, I reintroduce my design into nature."[30] Here we see "suicide as self-completion, as the only means of appropriately locating oneself in the 'design' of the cosmos."[31] For a culture that is increasingly unable to locate itself in the "design" of the cosmos, suicide may be increasingly attractive—especially when the instrument of suicide is simultaneously the prime symbol of secure order.

The myth of the hero reflects all of these positive aspirations contained in suicide, and another as well. Suicide, as Stengel mentions, is sometimes seen as a sort of spiritual test to determine the will of God: "Many suicidal attempts can even more aptly be compared with the *ordeal* . . . in its ancient ritual meaning; i.e., of a trial in which a person submitted himself, or was subjected, to a dangerous test the outcome of which was accepted as the judgment of the Deity."[32] When Fate is conceived as a deity, it may be Fate making the judgment. In the context of a more personal God, suicide may resemble the traditional Last-Judgment scene: "We all expect something of death, even if it's only damnation."[33]

The idea of suicide as ordeal leads to another relevant dimension of suicide—the dimension of risk and chance: "Most suicidal acts are manifestations of risk-taking behavior. They are gambles. . . . Uncertainty of outcome is not a contamination of the genuine suicidal act, but rather one of its inherent qualities."[34] As in the ordeal, this may be interpreted as a desire to test God or Fate and make it decide for or against the individual.[35] "Suicide may also be regarded as an experiment—a question which man puts to Nature, trying to force her to answer."[36] We have discussed previously the attraction of gambling, especially in a society that feels helpless in the face of Fate, and the intensity and excitement that it can generate. If the suicide is seeking a feeling of vitality and aliveness, the very act of putting one's life at risk without knowing the outcome may be the most vitalizing act of all. Yet to do this on a national and even global scale is, of course, much more exciting than doing it on a merely individual scale. Suicide has something of the air of Russian roulette about it, and the increasing rate of nuclear armament may easily be seen as a global Russian roulette. The risk of self-destruction may be seen as worthwhile, however, when no other access to equally intense experiences of power are available.

One of the important dimensions of the symbolism of nuclear weapons is the transcendence of time. The concern for eternity is also significant in suicide. One interpretation claims that "the person who commits suicide is one who . . . kills himself in order to place death under the control of the will. He opens up the possibility, in this paradoxical manner, of immortality; as though it were up to him whether he live or die; as though he chooses the time of death and could, had he so desired, not have died."[37] Suicide might thus be expected to increase when doubts about traditional affirmations of immortality increase: "It is not that the person who commits suicide really believes . . . that he is omnipotent. It is rather that there is some doubt in his mind. The doubt calls for proof. The proof is in the very fact that he can bring about his own death through an act of will."[38] Thus doubts about immortality may reflect doubts about power, and we have seen that the Bomb may easily be a symbol for laying to rest both sets of doubts, as suicide may be.

A number of writers have suggested that the crisis created by nuclear weapons is chiefly a crisis about immortality. Lifton's theory of psychic numbing centers on the Bomb's having taken away all our forms of symbolic immortality. Similarly, Anders notes that all forms of symbolic survival demand at least that the world around us survive, so that our memory has a "space" in which to survive. But "today our fear of death is extended to all of mankind; and if mankind were to perish leaving no memory in any being, engulfing all existence in darkness . . . everything will have been in vain, and there would be only that which had been, and nothing else. . . . Human mortality has acquired a new meaning—it is only today that its ultimate horror is brought home to us."[39] The Bomb, having created this absence of any meaningful sense of immortality, may also have created an increasingly intense desire for it; once again, the problem may come to be seen as the solution. If suicide may be seen as a paradoxical bid for immortality, then "mutual suicide" may certainly have the same meaning.

A wide variety of interpretations of suicide may thus be summed up under the categories that we have seen to be meaningful in understanding the impact of nuclear weapons. These weapons create the kinds of mental states that can produce the urge to suicide, and they can symbolize the kinds of rebirth and transformation toward which suicide is often directed. Yet this is of course paradoxical for, in fact, suicide, like the Bomb, creates neither new life, nor new power, nor eternity, but only death. Common sense, therefore, must press the question: Don't potential suicides realize this? Don't they see the impossibility of gaining any positive goal through suicide? If the interpretations just discussed strain our common sense, it may be necessary to face one final possibility. Let us suppose that those who contemplate suicide, either individual or nuclear and global, do in fact realize that it means the absolute end, total annihilation. Is it nevertheless possible that there is something desirable in this, which draws us to think about it seriously, prepare for it, and thus allow it to occur?

Suicide, as we have seen, often grows out of a sense of despair, which may in turn reflect a feeling of irreversible meaninglessness and absurdity. Emile Durkheim, in initiating the sociological study of suicide, suggested that some suicides are directly caused by anomie, the absence of an orderly and integrated worldview within which one can live. Earlier, we discussed at length the shattering terror that can be brought on by the loss of one's nomos. It is striking that in the very earliest years of the nuclear age an eminent psychiatrist pointed to this dimension of the impact of the new weapon. Franz Alexander wrote that the insecurity caused by the massively destructive new bomb was only quantitatively, but not qualitatively, different from the insecurity already endemic in

Western civilization. He described the various sources of insecurity, all of which revolved around the breakdown of traditional meaning structures, which led to increasing anomie, and then asserted that the threat of physical annihilation could not increase the prevalent insecurity very much more. In a sense, physical destruction would only be a material equivalent to the reversion to chaos that had already occurred on the social, cultural, and psychological levels. The sense of absurdity, which modern writers from Dostoevski to Camus had seen as the source of suicidal urges, could hardly be significantly heightened by the Bomb. The true psychological impact of the Bomb, Alexander claimed, was its appeal as a possible way out of this apparently impossible crisis. Sudden extinction might be seen as preferable to insecurity; "a painless end is more desireable than endless pain."[40]

This interpretation assumes that nuclear war would be the *big whoosh*—a flash of global cataclysm in which everything disappears instantly and painlessly. The lure of instantaneous extinction is pervasive in symbolic perceptions of the Bomb. Even a highly respected social scientist, Stanley Diamond, could say: "If *the* war should occur, the country will simply disappear some sunny day, while most of us are going about our apathetic business."[41] Of course, there is little likelihood that the end would be so simple for everyone. As George Wald put it: "You think, Bang!—and the next morning, if you're still there, you read in the newspapers that 50 million people were killed. But that isn't the way it happens." Referring to Hiroshima and Nagasaki victims, he went on to say: "A lot of them took a long time to die . . . millions of helpless, maimed, tortured and doomed survivors."[42] Yet once again we must turn aside from the empirical realities to examine the reality of symbolism. And the common perception of both suicide and nuclear war, among those whose common sense can not accept the myth of heroic survival, is likely to be the myth of the *big whoosh*.

Suicide seen as total extinction is the analogue on the individual level to the religious return to primal chaos in myth and ritual, as well as to the nuclear *big whoosh*. "The ordinary forms of suicide must stand as prototypes of acute generalized total self-destruction."[43] But our survey of theories of suicide corroborates our previous discussions of the appeal of voluntary annihilation: while the negative hope of escaping pain is a motivating factor, it is not nearly as significant as we might think. Rather, the appeal of extinction, even without an expectation of rebirth, is fundamentally positive. The common thread here has been recognized more readily by artists than psychologists. Leonardo da Vinci viewed the impulse to suicide as "the hope and desire of going back to primal chaos, like that of the moth to the light . . . this longing which in its quintessence is the spirit of the elements . . . and inherent in Nature."[44] Similarly, for Herman Hesse, suicides are those persons who "find the aim of life not in perfecting and molding of the self, but in liberating themselves by going back to the mother, back to God, back to the all. . . . They see death and not life as the releaser. They are ready to cast themselves away in surrender, to be extinguished and go back to the beginning."[45] From this point of view, suicides are drawn to intensify rather than oppose their situation—to take the apparently irreversible situation of anomie and make a virtue of its necessity by carrying it to its ultimate conclusion in perfect chaos. The satisfaction in doing so comes from much more than yielding to powerlessness and escaping pain.

In the fantasied *big whoosh* of suicide all the many-faceted attractions of transcending structure and dissolving in the limitless combine, luring the suicide to one final act of merger with the "all." Yet suicide offers more, for it holds out the promise of control; the suicide consciously creates, and thus gains power over, the primal chaos, death, and the infinite. Similarly, the Bomb offers the hope of one last moment of cosmic empowerment in the instant of global extinction. And it allows a suicide that is universally shared and consonant with the dominant values and worldview of our culture. Again we find that nuclear weapons offer themselves as the most appealing solution to the very problems they have created. Having led us to equate death with utter annihilation—having made us feel "dead in life"—they urge us to transcend this state. But transcendence turns out to mean the suicide of nuclear annihilation, "the only form of transcendence worthy of the age."[46]

Therefore, the vast majority of us do not seek out empirical knowledge of what nuclear war might be; in fact, we avoid such knowledge. It is much more appealing to rest content with the myth of the *big whoosh*, the one cosmic mushroom cloud in which all reality is instantly returned to the primordial chaos. Phrases such as "the end of civilization," "the end of human life," or even "the destruction of the planet" roll off our tongues easily. Is this not because we are in awe of such a possibility, fascinated as well as terrified, in the same way that we are drawn and simultaneously repelled by our own self-annihilation through transcendence? At a time in which most other avenues of transcendence seem blocked to us, are we willing to contemplate one great instant of permanent, self-induced transcendence? To flow up into the great mushroom cloud; to be filled with the unbelievable power of the atom; to explode the oppressive structures within us and around us; to take the final plunge, along with all humanity, into a cosmic unity; to return to the source from which all began. These are the deeply buried symbolic images that seduce us into following the Bomb, our modern God, down the path to the martyrdom of mutual suicide.

10

THE
DEATH-MACHINE
AS GOD

In the preceding chapters, I have suggested that above and beyond the reasons that nations offer publicly for nuclear armament there are other perhaps even more significant reasons, which have largely escaped public discussion; these can be discovered if we treat the Bomb as a symbol and study it as historians of religion study religious symbols. I have tried to show that the Bomb functions for us in many of the ways that symbols of sacrality function in other cultures and religious traditions. The primary such symbol in our tradition is, of course, God, and it may be at least plausible—and illuminating—to look at the Bomb quite literally as a form of, or substitute for, God.

The Bomb as God symbolizes awesome and limitless power, omniscience, eternity, and omnipresence, and allows us to feel a part of, or perhaps even in control of, those divine attributes. It symbolizes the sacred power that provides a coherent and enduring worldview and thus offers security, while simultaneously symbolizing the sacred as escape from structure, even though this entails our "creature-feeling" and insecurity. The Bomb symbolizes Fate and Chance and our powerlessness in the face of these divinities, which yet becomes power when we aquiesce to them. The Bomb as God makes our world and our lives appear unreal—as theater or as dream—when compared with its awesome power. The Bomb also symbolizes the irrationality that is inevitably an element in every experience of God.

The Bomb as God reflects the desire to return to primordial

chaos, which is so often a part of myths about the divine. Therefore it also symbolizes the new birth that comes from dissolution in chaos. In particular, it symbolizes the rebirth of the apocalyptic hero who, as God's agent or even as God himself, defeats the Enemy and purifies the world. The Bomb as God is the recipient of our sacrifices and the goal of our desire to unite with it in a sacred communion. And, finally, the Bomb symbolizes our desire to participate in divine power through the self-sacrifice of suicide, whether it brings us rebirth or not.

All of these themes have been part of our public and private lives since the beginning of the nuclear age. It would be mistaken, of course, to suggest that the Bomb's meanings have remained exactly the same over all that time. Certainly there have been changes, and eventually we shall have historical studies tracing those changes in detail. Those studies will probably show, among other things, that the symbolism of the Bomb falls into two distinct periods, the first from 1945 to 1963 and the second from the late 1970s onward. In between lies a fifteen-year period of relative public apathy toward the nuclear issue. In the first period, apocalyptic and heroic-rebirth themes were much in evidence, while in the second they are more in the background. In their place, we now see a greater stress on the dual-track image of deterrence and arms control. Yet images of confronting and defeating the Enemy are still widespread, accompanied by continuing concerns for national firmness, heroism, and renewal.

When some particular symbolic meanings come to the forefront of our consciousness, others recede. But all retain their hold over our unconscious thoughts and feelings, in the depths of the psyche where religious symbols have their true home. New images embrace rather than displace old ones; nothing is ever lost. Perhaps the clearest proof of this is the Strategic Defense Initiative, or "Star Wars" proposal, in which all the symbolic motifs of the nuclear age are tied together in one comprehensive package (which may well explain the plan's widespread popularity). So we can affirm that the symbolic meanings we have outlined here are the reservoir from which our most basic responses to the Bomb have always been and still are drawn.

These responses must therefore be seen as essentially religious responses. In talking about the Bomb we are talking about a God, and our speech is sacred speech or myth. In acting, in preparing for nuclear war and building up our nuclear arsenals, we are engaging in sacred behavior or ritual. And our speech itself is a form of ritual. Every society is loath to give up its God, its sacred symbols, its myths, and its rituals. We are no different. For in every respect, the symbolism of nuclear-weapons-as-God makes those weapons more appealing, more compelling, more desirable, more necessary to our lives. If we are to part with them, we must, as a first step, gain a clearer understanding of why we have not done so until now. But our study is not only a step on the path to averting catastrophe. For in a sense the catastrophe has already occurred. The very existence of thousands of nuclear warheads encircling the planet, even if they are never used, must have enormous impact upon the society and every individual in it. Even if an understanding of these weapons were to lead to total and permanent nuclear disarmament, we would still be compelled to live with the effects that they have had upon us psychologically, emotionally, and spiritually. In order to deal with those effects responsibly and constructively, we must understand them. For as long as nuclear weapons exist, and even after they no longer exist, we shall still be in their power until we have penetrated as deeply as possible into their symbolic meanings and the ways in which those meanings have reshaped individual and societal life.

The most comprehensive and significant approach to this problem so far has been Lifton's theory of psychic numbing. Anyone who gives Lifton's work a careful reading must admit that he has offered a compelling and illuminating concept, one that is able to explain a wide variety of contemporary phenomena and show clearly their links to the existence of nuclear weapons. Looking at the Bomb as a symbol has provided us with even further evidence to support his view. But at the same time, the Bomb has also appeared to symbolize realities that do not quite fit the theory of psychic numbing as the key to a total understanding of its effects. Therefore, we must look at a complex situation in which psychic numbing is related to other effects in a variety of ways. This should not be surprising, since it is clear that the Bomb, like all primary

religious symbols, can represent differing, conflicting, even contradictory realities simultaneously. Thus, as Lifton stresses, the Bomb
symbolizes death as total annihilation, utter extinction, an absolutely "broken connection" between death and the continuity of
life. But in seeing the Bomb as a symbol, it is clear that it may also
symbolize, in a wide variety of ways, renewed and eternal life,
vitality, power, meaningful order. The Bomb as symbol promises to
give precisely what it simultaneously takes away.

The copious evidence to support the theory of psychic numbing
and the equally copious evidence to support alternative views
suggest that neither one can be absolutely *the* correct or incorrect
view. Rather, each of us shares in both of these realities, in different
ways and to different degrees. But no one is able to escape the
effects of either aspect entirely. None of us can approach any
honesty about ourselves, our society, or our world unless we probe
as deeply and honestly as possible into the effects of nuclear
weapons upon our lives. If there is any hope that as individuals and
as a society we can escape the chaotic absurdity of the present, put
the pieces of our world back together in a coherent and meaningfully unified worldview, we must take account of nuclear weapons.
They form a "piece" of our worldview that is crucially important,
although we have consistently trained ourselves to deny this.

The similarities between the Bomb and other religious realities
tell us part of what we need to know. But we must also ask how our
new God differs from all previous gods, for only then can we see
clearly how it affects us in unprecedented ways. One point, which
has been implicit in our previous discussion, must now be brought
out explicitly: this God is a machine, a technological device
invented by human beings. Yet the machine, being infinitely more
powerful than the humans who invented it, has become a Franken-
stein's Monster, independent of its creators and capable of turning
violently upon them. And "them" is now, of course, all of us. We
have the choice of either cooperating or resisting when the machine
acts; because of its many appealing symbolic qualities, we generally
cooperate. We become partners in the machine's actions and thus,
in a very real sense, parts of the machine. We are all soldiers in the
front-line trenches, but the Bomb is our commander and we do its
bidding. This is especially clear in the concept of MAD; the citizens

of all superpowers become linked together in a single machine, which demands more and more sacrifices; the actions of one side must (according to this theory) necessarily evoke corresponding actions from the other side.

The way in which we prepare for war reflects and foreshadows the way we shall wage war: "In a push-button war involving nuclear missiles, there will be no direct contact between adversaries. The techniques of war are fast becoming as impersonal and mechanized as pulling a lever to start a production chainbelt. In such a setting, the best soldier is not the 'hero' but the 'automaton.' "[1] We voluntarily become automatons, mere parts of a machine, in part because of our age-old mythic dream of being heroes and our mythic desire to embody in ourselves the power inherent in the divine machine. What Moss says of the Strategic Air Command bomber pilot may be true for all of us: "He is equally remote from the human will that makes a decision on using or not using the bomb, and the human suffering that its use would cause. He sees himself as part of a complex instrument, an agent between someone else's will and its effect, a living button. His pride is to function in this role perfectly. He has a sense of importance."[2] Ultimately, though, in our symbolic perception, it may very well be the Bomb itself whose will we obey, for how can any human will dare to interfere with that of the divine? Even the greatest national leaders are merely parts of the machine. And, as we have seen, our importance becomes not merely social or political, but in fact sacred and cosmic in scope.

At the same time, psychic numbing reinforces the pattern effected by symbolic meaning. For if we are in fact "dead in life," already suffused with the death taint of the Bomb, then it is that much easier to see ourselves as machines and to take pride in being perfectly functioning machines. Of course, this sense of the mechanization of human life was hardly created by the nuclear age. Here, as in so many other instances, the Bomb is both a reflection and a shaper of our relationship with reality. But the elevation of a machine to a central place in our symbolic world—the deification of a machine—surely makes it much more likely that we shall see ourselves as automatons. Moreover, the technologically induced problem offers itself as a solution. As this machine God intensifies our psychic numbing, we seek to escape that numbing by finding meaning in a symbolic form of immortality that is itself technological, as Lifton suggests: "Everyone in this age participates in a sense of immortality derived from the interlocking human projects we call science and technology."[3] Thus, as technology absorbs those provinces of life that were previously considered spiritual, it may be fair to say that technology has become the soul of the body of humanity.[4]

Yet we cannot be totally content with being machines. In fact, as we saw previously, the existentialist movement may be said to have started with Dostoevski's revolt against being a mere piano key, a part of a machine. The sense of dehumanization and the sheer boredom—the flatness of life—which afflicts automatons can be challenged only in situations of great intensity. Russian roulette may easily become, as in the film *The Deer Hunter*, a primary symbol for the modern world's escape from the dehumanization of a technological God. The intensity of risk is combined with the joy of being entertained in a theater of life-and-death. But for the ultimate "kick," the stakes must be ultimately high. Thus the machine deity leads us to give ourselves over to it in a game of global Russian roulette in which we all hold the pistol. And apparently we do so willingly.

Machines must inevitably see all the world as a machine: "The more a man acts on the basis of a self-image that assumes he is powerless, an impotent cog in a huge machine, the more likely he is to drift into a pattern of dehumanized thinking and action toward others."[5] "We have become masters of the impersonal and the inanimate. Our energy and even our emotions have gone into things; the things serve us but come between us, changing the relationship of man to man. And the things take on an authority that men accept without protest. The impersonality is epidemic. It is almost as though we feared direct contact, almost as though the soul of man had become septic."[6] Thus we find our identity not by relating to other individuals as individuals, but by seeing ourselves merely as a part of "the crowd" or "the nation," whose emblem and savior is the Bomb, the ultimate machine. We lose the subtleties and nuances of human complexity and see the world in absolutes, "us versus them." We view human relationships in terms of the mythic, apocalyptic vision, a vision whose ultimate promise is the annihilation of "their" machine and unlimited license for "our" machine to do whatever it wants.

In fact, the ultimate goal of machine people is always to have total dominance, unlimited autonomy to manipulate the environment—both human and natural—in endless technological ways. Thus the machine God also shapes our relationship with our physical and material environment, leading us to the environmental crisis that we now face. Again, the fouling of the air, water, and land was hardly begun in the nuclear age, but the symbolism of the Bomb makes it much more difficult to escape from this predicament too. Behind our callousness toward the natural realm there is not only a desire for quick and easy profit, but a more fundamental view of ourselves as radically separated from nature. In the battle of the machines to dominate the elements, we are clearly on the side of the machines—we are the machines—and this battle is seen in radically dualistic, even apocalyptic, terms. Thus, having no meaningful relationship with nature, we are free, perhaps even compelled, to manipulate it endlessly. The transformation of raw materials into manufactured goods thus becomes our primary goal and value; if the Bomb is God, then the GNP is chief of the angels.

Yet our commitment to material goods as highest good may have a more complex significance. It is fostered not only by the symbol of the Bomb as divine controller, manipulator, and dominator, but also by the psychic numbing that the Bomb creates. If we dare not think about the true reality of our lives—the sword of Damocles that constantly threatens total extinction at a moment's notice—then we must divert ourselves, making the other, numbed level so complex and interesting that we shall not have time to think about the truth. And we must make ourselves so comfortable that we shall not care to deal with the danger. Thus the Bomb and the economy are interlocked not only from a strictly economic point of view (though most people do believe that more bombs are good for the economy, despite the doubts raised by economists), but also from the psychological and symbolic standpoints.

The Bomb, the economy, and our lives all form parts of one interlocking machine, offering us enough satisfactions that we refuse to ask about the deeper meaning of the machine's life. When this question threatens to arise, the diversions of life as theater of the absurd and global Russian roulette are there to entertain us and soothe our doubts. Thus we desperately desire the security that we hope to gain from total domination and manipulation of our world, but we simultaneously demand the insecurity that will make life interesting and entertaining. And we certainly get this insecurity, for we have based our hopes of security on a God that, as we have seen, cannot provide it. We hope to dominate the Enemy with a weapon that by its very nature cannot offer the freedom that we seek through domination. We are caught in a vicious circle in which the quest for security can only breed the anxiety of insecurity. But machines can't feel anxiety, so it may be easier, for this reason too, to live as a machine.

Finally, then, we come to treat not only the natural world and our fellow human beings as machines, but ourselves as well. We offer ourselves, our thoughts and feelings, to the machine and the nation that embodies it, and we perceive those feelings and thoughts as parts of the unreality that surrounds us: "Faced with the prospect of the destruction of mankind, we feel neither violent nor guilty, as though we were all involved in a gigantic delusion of negation of the external as well as of our internal reality."[7] We allow ourselves to be numbed, finding it the easiest way to cope with an impossible situation, and thus we commit "partial suicide," which in turn allows us to continue preparing for total suicide on a global scale. We commit ourselves to a machine that is infinitely violent and must wreak its violence on us if it is to be used on others. Therefore, as much as we fear the Enemy, we must fear ourselves in equal measure, and this fear of ourselves reinforces the numbing.

So we find powerlessness attractive, even as we chase the delusion of ultimate power, for we know that this dream of ultimate power is ultimately suicidal and thus we want to perceive ourselves as weak—incapable of, or at least not responsible for, pushing the button. Caught in this contradiction, along with so many others, we escape by immersing ourselves in the air of unreality, of craziness, surrounding it all, and thus the circle is completed: at every turn, the symbolism of the Bomb as God, which makes nuclear weapons so attractive to us, reinforces the tendency toward numbing, and numbing reinforces our commitment to the Bomb as God.

A similar dialectical interaction is evident when we turn to the other unique feature of the Bomb as God: while all other gods are seen as sources of death, they are also sources of life. Only in our own day has a God appeared that is capable of providing death but not life. The (often unconscious) awareness of this characteristic lies at the heart of psychic numbing. But psychic numbing is in many respects intolerable. Its victims are unwilling, perhaps unable, to admit its existence, and they may even be driven to suicide in order to escape from it. Since the Bomb, which could create no new symbols of a meaningful future itself, had been born out of a context of old symbols of hope and continuity, and since psychic numbing can be escaped only by grasping onto such symbols no matter how desperately, the old symbols were grafted onto the Bomb and defined much of its meaning. Most crucially, the very nature of the Bomb—its "Godlike" qualities—made it immensely suitable to be the bearer and focus of these traditional, essentially religious, symbols. Hence the fundamental ambivalence of the Bomb: it creates, enhances, and embodies the sense of death as utter extinction, which produces psychic numbing, but at the very same time it offers itself as a symbol of continuing life, a cure for the numbing, and its offer is largely accepted.

At every point of our discussion, we have seen that the Bomb offers meaning in the way that traditional symbols of the sacred once did, but it simultaneously betrays that offer and fails to deliver on its promise. It promises unlimited power but renders us powerless. If offers unshakable security but demands that we pay the price of insecurity. It leads us toward an experience of absolute reality but demands that we live lives of dreamlike (or nightmarish) unreality. It speaks to us of a context of apparent order and rationality, but it plunges us into lives of disorderly irrationality. It lures us with visions of unalterable destiny and yet compels us to accept capricious Chance. It gives us the illusion of controlling its power and thus the chance to play God, while it actually controls us and forces us to accept it as our God. And, perhaps most crucially, the Bomb claims to offer us, through its many symbolic meanings, new life, even eternal life; but it demands of us sacrifice on an unprecedented scale—the ultimate sacrifice of global suicide—and it fails to give back any glimmer of life in return.

The Bomb as God is, to sum it up bluntly, a cruel hoax. Yet in a sense it is a brilliant and brilliantly successful hoax. We fail to see through the hoax for two reasons. First, the Bomb in its guise of God has a wide variety of appeals. It allows us to keep alive our traditional embrace of the symbolisms that it embodies; it helps us to hide from the truth that we don't want to see. And second, the Bomb in its true identity of ultimate annihilator numbs us, so that we are mentally and emotionally frozen and unable to see what we ought to see. Thus the Bomb as a symbol of new life and the Bomb as a source of utter extinction—and hence psychic numbing—can be one and the same Bomb, its two sides reinforcing each other to this very day.

Having explored the two unique qualities of our new God, we can now turn to the essential question of the relationship between these two qualities. Is it merely coincidence that a society that created a machine as God happened to create a machine of destruction and death? Or, is there some intrinsic connection between these two unique properties of our unholy God? It is not likely to be coincidence, for there is a logical path that leads from technology to destruction.

Fundamentally, the machine represents, as we have suggested, the human attempt to manipulate and dominate the environment. From the eighteenth to the early twentieth centuries, there was a widespread optimism in Western civilization that this attempt would be successful. "Progress," inevitable and unlimited, was the order of the day. Progress meant that we, in cooperation with our machines, could increasingly conquer disease, famine, injustice, all sorts of disorder and suffering—and ultimately, at least by implication, death itself. A realm of perfect order and infinite life became not just a mythic vision but an aspiration that could be brought into historical reality through the rational organization of human and technological resources. Death and disorder thus became the Enemy, and victory in this final war seemed eminently possible.

The symbolic universe of ancient and medieval times, which was here being overthrown, was quite different. It accepted the inevitability of death, suffering, and disorder, until God himself put an apocalyptic end to them. As long as humans tried to eradicate these ills with merely human methods, they would necessarily fail. Thus the traditional vision saw a place for evil, even a positive place; we have seen how the apocalyptic vision gave these evils an important role in the scheme of cosmic history. Just as the god Death in Canaanite myth must periodically be yielded victories and given his due, so his embodiments in the historical realm must be accepted and endured as part of God's plan, according to Jewish, Christian, and Muslim views (and the view of virtually all other religious traditions as well).

In this perspective, modern Western culture appears unique, a noble experiment to see whether a culture could face the "terror of history," not by placing it in a mythological framework that accepted it as inevitable (albeit temporary) but by attacking it head-on with technology. The corollary to this was, of course, a greatly intensified fear of suffering, disorder, and especially death. They no longer had a meaningful place in the environment; they were foreign intrusions, which were there only to be wiped out. And, as the Enemy, they were to be both hated and feared. The lure of the human being as machine was thus the lure of identifying oneself with one's only weapon against the Enemy; if we all became machines, how much more potent the machine would be and how much more rapid our victory. In the twentieth century, many Europeans and an increasing number of Americans have raised serious questions about this technological panacea. But its legacy lives on in our inability to accept disorder and death, our incapacity to see them as anything other than the threatening Enemy.

Yet we ended up with death, the Enemy, as our God. Why? Psychologists might suggest that the answer lies in the "return of the repressed." A technological society that intends to eliminate disorder and death in the environment must also deny the fascination these experiences exert on the psyche. This fascination will not disappear, however, so it must be repressed into unconsciousness. It becomes the inner Enemy. Psychoanalytic theories suggest, in a variety of ways, that this inner Enemy will inevitably find a way out. In our thoughts, fantasies, and actions we shall project the re-pressed parts of the mind into our environment, while claiming that we hope to remove them. The more we repress, the larger the projections become. In this light, the Bomb appears as a massive projection of that inner dimension of disorder and destruction that we consistently deny. It gives us a mirror in which we can avoid seeing ourselves, so that we need not recognize the distasteful aspects of who and what we really are. As this projection becomes larger and larger, and as we become more and more overwhelmed by it, it is easier and easier to avoid honest self-awareness. Eventually we come to worship this projection. The Bomb as God gives the fullest expression of our unconscious fascination with death, while giving the fullest repression of that fascination into the depths of unconsciousness, where it need not trouble the professed values of technological progress.

But it was not only the "dark side" within us that was repressed. More fundamentally, it was our need for a vision of the wholeness of reality, a vision that would include symbols of the link between life and death, creation and destruction, good and evil. We have seen at length that wholeness—with its concomitant sense of transcending limits through a coincidence of opposites—is a central aspect of all religious symbolism, including the symbolic meanings of the Bomb. Many modern interpreters of religion would suggest that this kind of unlimitedness is in fact the defining characteristic of authentic religious experience. Among these, one of the most persuasive and influential is the theologian Paul Tillich. Tillich's thought sheds an interesting light on the relationship between technology and death in the modern world.

Modern technology, Tillich claims, has made us masters of the parts of our lives. We have learned to analyze and manipulate the specific pieces of our world in an astounding variety of ways. These successes lead us to focus exclusively on the "limited" in our experiences, our values, our goals. So we become internally divided and limited: a part of each of us values material comfort and works for it; a part values intellectual understanding and works for it. A part of us values excitement in life and works for it; a part values tranquil contentment and works for it. Each of these parts may be satisfied, Tillich points out, but as each goal is attained, something within us still remains unfulfilled. So we set out in quest of some new goal, only to find that, having achieved it, we still feel dissatisfied. Every achievement is a means to some further achievement, but there is no ultimate end or purpose—no goal that can promise total fulfillment.

We are like the cat, endlessly chasing its own tail and never stopping to ask why. In fact, technology may prohibit us from asking the meaning of the whole. Not only does it direct our attention away from wholeness and symbols of wholeness, it actually denies the validity or possibility of any unified meaning at all. Our technical triumphs have created the most successful production-and-consumption machine in the history of the world. But we are unable to step outside the machine and ask about its ultimate meaning, for we are parts of the machine. We are means for other means, none of which have any ultimate end except to keep the machine—as pointless as it may be—functioning. Trapped inside this machine, we cannot get enough perspective to see it in its wholeness and ask the question of meaning. Perhaps we dare not ask. Like jugglers, we try to keep the many distinct and often conflicting pieces of our lives in constant motion. If we stopped even for a moment to ask the ultimate purpose of all our activity, all the pieces might very well come tumbling down upon us. Many people avoid this potentially disastrous question by treating some limited value as if it were of unlimited worth (e.g., their nation's political and military power). To still their own nagging doubts, they must silence those who question their choices—with a Bomb, if necessary.

Tillich's analysis points us to the further conclusion that there may in fact be an overarching purpose in our society: avoiding the question of the meaning and purpose of the whole. As long as we can immerse ourselves in the comforts of our radically finitized life, we can evade the whole issue of ultimate meaning. We evade it because we fear the emptiness of a life that has no answer for it. We evade it, too, because the breakdown of traditional religious structures has left us bereft of meaningful symbols to link us to the whole of reality. An encounter with totality can be a shattering experience; without viable symbols to make it endurable, it can seem to be an encounter with absolute nothingness. Were we to risk such an encounter, we would come face to face with the Bomb as our only symbol of ultimacy and we would have to recognize all of its disturbing implications. It is easier to take refuge in a partial reality suffused with unreality, to fall back into the numbed apathy of acquiescence in meaninglessness. So we may actually prize our meaninglessness. Ignoring the meaning of life, we can ignore the meaning of death as well and continue to believe it devoid of meaning.

Implicitly, though, we are affirming that if life has no ultimate meaning then death is as meaningful as life. And perhaps we actually see death as even more meaningful than life, for death may be the ideal image toward which technological life leads us. As we surrender to the machine, seeing our only meaning as servants who must keep the machine running smoothly, we merge into the machine and lose the sense of being truly alive. The ultimate end of this process might be called the total "thingification" of reality— the reduction of all life to meaningless inert objects. Though we keep up our belief in the fight against death, this Enemy actually becomes our best image of a totally fragmented and purposeless world. "Things fall apart. The center cannot hold." These words of the poet Yeats describe the process of technology leading us further and further into the disintegration of values and meanings. The total dissolution provided by death seems to be our ultimate goal. "Death in life" may be less our fear than our aspiration. The more we try to deny this aspiration, the more we become unconsciously obsessed with it. Finally it dominates our lives. While we seem to employ our limited and scattered energies fighting against this Enemy, it actually grows to be an unlimited and all-engulfing whole. Denied wholeness in life, may we not seek it in death, that mirror image of what our world is striving to become?

It is but a short step further to the divinization of death. Like the devil of traditional religion, every Enemy has an air of sacrality about it. That air is greatly enhanced when the Enemy represents the infinitude that we are denied. Having stripped life of its sacred power through our technological control of it, we may now find sacred power only in death. The process is completed when the Enemy suddenly merges with the God on whom we relied to vanquish it. Death and technology merge completely in the Bomb—

and we, overwhelmed with awe, have no choice but to fall on our knees and worship.

It is understandable that in a world without wholeness, a world that radically separates life and death, God would be seen as a source of either life or death, but not both. We have just seen that in such a world it is likely, perhaps inevitable, that a death-giving God would come to the fore, particularly if that God is a technological machine. But at the same time, such a world fosters the desire for wholeness in equal measure as it takes the actuality of wholeness away. Thus a death-God easily becomes a symbol of hoped-for wholeness, since no other is available, and it draws to itself symbols of life, no matter how illusory the wholeness and life it claims to offer. Moreover, the numbing such a God engenders fosters, as we have seen, a willingness to accept illusory wholeness—an illusory unity of life and death—precisely because the real experience of such unity is no longer available.

The success of a death-God is further enhanced because a loss of wholeness means a loss of traditional symbols of wholeness. Those traditional symbols no longer seem able to deliver on their promise; they lose their meaning and hence their very life for increasing numbers of people in an age of secularization. There is a search for new symbols that can take their place. But the Bomb, as a source of psychic numbing, makes it virtually impossible for new meaningful symbols to grow and find acceptance; and then the Bomb, as illusory symbol of wholeness, offers itself as the one available solution to the problem of the age. Thus the Bomb absorbs and negates whatever attempts might be made to find new, positive religious imagery.

The trap it sets is rather like a maze; each time we move toward a positive vision of life, we find that the Bomb has preceded us there and already linked itself to that vision. Thus we set off in another direction, but soon enough find that the Bomb has beaten us to it there as well. We wander from spiritual and symbolic place to place, trying to find a place in which we can establish ourselves firmly to oppose the hoax of the Bomb, but it seems that such places no longer exist. The Bomb is indeed omnipresent; that is one promise of the divine on which it does deliver. And its manifold inner contradictions—its offer of life and promise of death, its constant answer of "Yes and No" to all of our deepest life-questions—even enhance its appearance as a symbol of wholeness. The power of a religious symbol, as we have often noted, lies largely in its paradoxical ability to embody opposites simultaneously, and surely in this regard the Bomb is as potent a symbol as any. Thus it is no valid critique of the Bomb merely to point out its fundamentally contradictory nature. Rather, to our religious selves, which are largely unconscious selves, it confirms our suspicion that in the Bomb we have found our true God.

Epilogue

TOWARD THE
FOURTH LEVEL

It is hard to be optimistic when thinking about nuclear weapons. For many years writers on the subject have pointed to the apparently insoluble dilemma that confronts even the most optimistic natures: in the nuclear age, we must live on two levels. On the first, we are to some degree aware of the threat of nuclear annihilation, and this leaves us terribly pessimistic. So we turn away to the second level, the level of psychic numbing, on which we deny the threat and go about our ordinary business as if it did not exist. But the longer we deny the threat, the longer we fail to remove it; recognizing our failure makes us even more pessimistic. Now we see that there is yet a third level—the level on which we maintain nuclear weapons because of their appealing symbolic meanings.

Exploring this third level, we have apparently discovered that we are trapped. At every turn our conclusions seem to bar the way to any optimism about the future. And so, finally, we must ask the most difficult question: Is there any way out of this trap, this maze in which the Bomb seems to have ensnared us? Or are we destined to wander through its labyrinthine psychological twists and turns until the symbol explodes its final reality upon us?

If we are to find a way out, we must start with an honest awareness of the true depth of our problem. First, we must recognize that there are in fact three, not two, levels that must be dealt with. Then we must understand as fully as possible the complex relationships, both of cooperation and of conflict, among these three levels. Our discussion thus far has provided some sense of what these relationships are. The first two levels seem to be mutually exclusive; we can go from awareness to numbing and back again, but it is extremely difficult, if not impossible, to link them in an integrated whole. The level of symbolic meanings interacts in a huge variety of ways with both these levels. The most basic pattern may be the conspiracy between the symbolic level and the level of numbing. But we have seen that the partners in this conspiracy have conflicts themselves and live somewhat uneasily together.

Living on all three of these levels, we experience their tensions and conflicts as our own. As long as the Bomb exists, it seems unlikely that any of these three levels will disappear, and it is equally unlikely that they can be reconciled. Their uneasy coexistence will continue to dwell in each of us, and we shall be forced to live now on one, now on another, never reconciling all three in a true harmony. Thus we shall suffer from the Bomb in a myriad of ways even if it is never again used. On each of the three levels, nuclear weapons fragment our lives and rob us of the wholeness we so desperately desire. The conflicts among these levels then compound the damage and wound our inner lives even more. This is the true depth of our problem.

But perhaps, having recognized this painful truth, we need not sink back into despair. Perhaps we can recognize that there is a way out, a way that awaits us if we will choose it. To escape from the trap that has ensnared us all, we can create and explore still another level on which we look with full honesty at the other three and their effects on our lives. This fourth level must take full account of all our present reality, as well as opening a door to new future realities. Otherwise it will be merely another fragment of our fragmented lives, another partial level in conflict with those on which we already live. The fourth level must include and yet transcend the other three, finding room for all their elements, bringing them all to full consciousness, yet transforming them into a harmonious synthesis. The honesty it demands may well be painful. Giving up our numbed state means letting ourselves feel—feel the full terror of what the Bomb might someday do and the full craziness of what it has already done to us. Yet the only alternative is to continue the numbing, the craziness, the wound of inner schism, and the increasing risk that one day all of it will end in a reality that will force upon us the honesty we so long avoided.

The need for total honesty is pressed upon us from another direction as well. If our goal is to transcend the fragmentation and partial reality of the modern technological world, to attain a sense of wholeness and fulfillment in our lives, we must become whole people in the very process; the means must suit the end. Technology seems to demand that knowledge be a partial thing. As the philosopher Martin Buber has shown, "knowledge" today is usually equated with that analytical "I–It" knowledge that splits its object into qualities, features, and aspects. It demands only the rational, analytical part of our minds, and so it demands that we withhold the total fullness of our beings from the objects that we wish to know. If we come to the issue of nuclear weapons with only this kind of knowledge in mind, we shall merely further enhance the fragmented state of our minds and our lives. If we hope to transcend this state and find some kind of wholeness, we must begin by bringing a kind of wholeness to our search.

In Buber's view, the way to do this is to "imagine the real," to put ourselves so totally and completely in the place of that which we wish to know that it becomes totally real to us. This does not mean that we must give up our own individuality and identity. Buber asserts that in this kind of "I–Thou" knowing we remain totally ourselves yet simultaneously become fully identified with the object of our knowledge. If we fail to do this—if we bring only part of ourselves to the relationship—we know only a part of what lies before us. If, on the other hand, we "imagine the real," we have the privilege and the obligation of knowing the object in its full and therefore its genuine reality. The longer we hide behind partial knowledge to falsify the world, the longer we are trapped in a world of limited and partial reality. Only "imagining the real" can provide a way out of this trap. And this demands that we confront the real and full horror of nuclear weapons.

In some sense, this process is already under way. In the 1980s, for the first time, the public has had access to substantial information about the empirical realities of nuclear war. If we choose, we can (like the biblical prophets) experience the coming apocalypse in vivid detail. Only a few choose to bear this painful burden. But many absorb at least enough information to falsify fantasy images. It is increasingly difficult to maintain the vision of "heroic rebirth" in the face of accumulating evidence that the vision has little resemblance to the likely reality. It is equally difficult to hope for the painless universal obliteration of the *big whoosh*, as the evidence suggests that many millions would suffer long lingering death over weeks, months, or even years. Only a minimum of accurate information is needed to comprehend the reality that belies these fantasies. And even this minimum can help us to break out of the level of psychic numbing. As Lifton puts it, "This seemingly new information makes contact with amorphous, menacing fears that have been suppressed by the numbing process. Now these fears are named, and the images that have the ring of truth are presented forthrightly; however grim the images, the effect is liberating."[1]

Fragmentary facts about nuclear war liberate us by moving us momentarily to the level of honest awareness and strengthening our desire for further awareness. But as this desire grows, it must confront the overriding truth that there is no absolute truth about the effects of nuclear weapons. As more research proceeds and more facts accumulate, the data become more complex, more bewildering, and more quickly overwhelming. The one fact that stands out is that no one knows with certainty what a full-scale nuclear war would actually be like. Because it is a totally unprecedented phenomenon, there are no meaningful models available. Most researchers on the subject suggest that the reality would be worse than their projections, because the destructive effects would be cumulative and synergistic. But they cannot be sure. When we try to "imagine the real" as we contemplate nuclear war, we quickly find that the dependable border between empirical reality and inner fantasy dissolves. If there is no empirical certainty, we cannot rely on our reality testing to restrain or contradict our fantasies. So whatever we imagine about nuclear war must take us beyond the bounds of literal reality.

Even if scientific research could provide an absolutely verifiable, empirical picture of nuclear war and its results, it is doubtful whether we would or could accept it merely as objective information. We have seen that the Bomb, with its immense power, inevitably stirs up ambiguous responses that can be expressed only in symbolic terms. We have seen that even the "experts," the scientists and strategists, cannot remain within the confines of literal language and perhaps do not wish to. This is hardly surprising. Warfare has always been mythologized, from the battles of the ancient warrior gods to the images in which we recall the two world wars. Yet nuclear war would go far beyond any of these in its intensity and scope, so it must demand the language of symbol and myth. Regardless of the status of scientific research, our powers of reality testing will probably always fail in the face of a threat of global catastrophe. Our perceptions of the nuclear issue may therefore always take us into a psychological realm where reality and fantasy merge.

Moreover, even if we could imagine the reality of nuclear war in purely literal terms, there is good reason to believe that we should not follow this path. Literal thinking and literal language impose a particular mode of thought and feeling, one that is intimately linked with the Bomb and its symbolism. Literalism insists that in every situation there is one single meaning and one single truth to be found. Thus it divides the world into true and false, right and wrong, good and evil, with no middle ground allowed. It is the characteristic language of a culture bent on an apocalyptic crusade to wipe out all evil. It allows no ground for a unified vision of good and evil or life and death together. At the same time, literalism underscores our psychic numbing. With its statistics, computer projections, and abstract theoretical models, the literal approach reduces the world to a set of finite means and ends, each with a single simple meaning. It fails to grasp the complexities of human reality and human response. It creates a dehumanized world, amenable to manipulation and control, in which we learn to see other people and ultimately ourselves as mere inert objects. It is the characteristic language of a technological culture that has made a death-machine its deity.

The inert words of literalism create an inert world, in which every thing is just the thing it is and can be nothing else. In this one-dimensional world it is increasingly difficult to give possible realities and imagined realities any meaningful place. So we are prevented by our mode of speaking and thinking from exploring genuine alternatives to the existing situation. We are also prevented from recognizing the reality and power of our symbolisms and fantasies. Since we define literal truth as the only valid form of truth, we deny that our unconscious processes have any valid truth at all. So literalism becomes part of the process of psychological repression. This is especially dangerous in the nuclear age, when the difference between literal reality and fantasy is so hard to find. With fantasy images affecting us so powerfully, we must exert ever more powerful processes of repression. One way to achieve this is simply to intensify our numbing—to refuse to feel at all. Another way is to project our inner thoughts and feelings onto external objects—to make the Enemy responsible for all the anger and hatred and dark feeling that wells up inside us. As numbing reinforces our commitment to dehumanizing technology, projection reinforces our commitment to the apocalyptic crusade against the Enemy. So literalism again ties together both our ways of thinking about the Bomb and our efforts to avoid thinking about it.

Yet even the most ardent literalism cannot banish the symbolic dimensions of our minds and our symbolic responses to the Bomb. Indeed, our conviction that literal truth is the only truth paradoxically strengthens the grip of symbolic meanings. The more literalism starves our supply of symbolic thinking and feeling, the more it feeds our hunger, and the more intensively we cling to our symbols. Since we are convinced that these nuclear symbols are actually literal realities, they take even deeper root in our psyches. When warnings of the dire reality of nuclear war are cast in purely literal terms, they are received on the symbolic level (even if we consciously deny this) and their threatening aspect is largely nullified.

Perhaps this explains, in part, the relatively limited success of the nuclear disarmament movement. The movement has tried to move us from the level of numbing to the level of awareness by urging us to imagine the literal horrors of nuclear war. Yet its alarms have fallen largely on deaf ears. The movement itself has explained this deafness by pointing to the conflict between the first two levels of awareness and numbing. But in its commitment to literal thinking it has ignored the third level of symbolic meaning. This literalism is just part of a larger picture—the disarmament movement's roots in the liberal humanism of the eighteenth-century Enlightenment.

This rationalistic humanism strips the issue of its religious and psychological complexities and sees it as a purely ethical matter: humanism and life against global death, one value against another. It assumes that ethical problems must be resolved by literal factual analysis and clear logical analysis alone. It assumes, furthermore, that all people are rational and can be shown the convergence of morality and self-interest. Therefore the movement puts all its energies into education based solely on facts and logical arguments. Yet it is clear that the nuclear issue goes beyond ethical considerations, and it is equally clear that the antinuclear campaign cannot succeed merely by stressing the irrationality of nuclear armament, for the Bomb's nonrational symbolic meanings lie at the heart of its appeal. Moreover, the Enlightenment tradition still links its faith in rationality to a belief in "progress," which means the triumph of the forces of life over the forces of death.

Yet all these Enlightenment values are the very values held just as fervently by nuclear policymakers, strategists, and political and military leaders. We have seen ample evidence that they too put their faith in logical analysis and the triumph of life over death, always holding the opposites apart. And proponents of nuclear armament have always couched their arguments in the most literal terms. The media have largely accepted this literal treatment and passed it along to the general public. Media presentations of the issue have been saturated with symbolic meanings that have gone unrecognized as symbolism because we have assumed that all truth must be literal truth. So the disarmament movement's own roots are closely intertwined with the roots of the very tree it hopes to fell. As long as it fails to recognize the role of symbolism and the irrational in the psyche, it will fail to grasp the fascinating, appealing qualities of the Bomb. If we are to "imagine the real," the first step is to understand that the reality we must imagine is largely a symbolic reality that crosses the line between literalism and fantasy.

The second step is to learn to deal with symbolism in its own language. We cannot "imagine the real" completely, or even primarily, in literal terms. Literalism is the language of "I–It" detachment; the reality we must imagine demands an attitude of "I–Thou" engagement, with a sensitive respect for the ambiguity and mystery of ultimate questions. So it is counterproductive to suggest that we strip away the symbolic meanings we have uncovered here, as if they were merely some superfluous camouflage hiding the truth. If one symbolism is stripped away, another will grow to takes its place. Rather, we must strip away the literalism that camouflages symbolic truth; we must "realize the imagined." Then we can proceed to find new symbolic meanings that can more fruitfully nourish a safe and satisfying life. The fourth level must be created not by *de*symbolizing but by *re*symbolizing.

Symbolism has its dangers too. If our goal is to confront the full reality of nuclear war, every symbol and every mythic image may tend to lead us further away by masking that reality. Surely those who attempt to "imagine the real" must be aware of the pitfalls on both sides of their path. They must assimilate empirical information with full awareness of the tendency to mythicize it and to dehumanize it, while they must absorb symbolic images of nuclear war with full awareness of the temptation to avoid the truth and its horror. The fourth level demands a sensitive use of both literal and symbolic language. Ideally, a new language may be needed, which synthesizes both approaches and teaches us how to weave them together most effectively in the pursuit of wholeness. Only with such a new language could we confront the phenomenon on both conscious and unconscious levels and unite the two into a single perception. This new mode of thought and speech is probably a distant reality. But its raw materials can be created today. While the disarmament movement is pressing ahead with increasingly precise facts on the empirical side, there is still much to be done in creative exploration of the symbolic side.

The best place to begin is, as always, where we are now. Having analyzed the existing symbolism, we may let it point us toward the possibility of new symbols. Having examined the interactions among the three existing levels, we may let those interactions point us toward the fourth level. Perhaps it will turn out that little really new is needed. The task may be one of simply seeing what already exists and then rearranging those perceptions and giving them a new shape.

Our acceptance of nuclear weapons points to the obvious starting place. Because these weapons are symbols of sacrality, they are clear evidence that we have not lost our desire for contact with the sacred. They continue to exist largely because we still desire the experience of numinous power, the awe and terror and fascination that it brings. We still desire the sense of eternity, the rebirth into new life. We still desire some kind of unified worldview, an unshakable source of meaning based on and supporting these religious experiences. And we desire the wholeness that power and meaning-structure have traditionally provided; thus we still insist on finding a single symbol that can embody all these aspects of our spiritual need and—more importantly—bring them together in a synthesis that is paradoxical and yet, for that very reason, even more fulfilling.

As we discover that the Bomb cannot truly satisfy these desires, we simultaneously discover and reaffirm to ourselves that the desires are still very much alive within us; perhaps they are even heightened by a symbol that promises to fulfill them but is unable to do so. They are, to be sure, numbed and repressed in a world that is unable to offer them satisfaction. But they still exist and may be awakened to full intensity again. To build the fourth level means to build a symbolic world in which these religious aspirations can be truly fulfilled and a true wholeness can be attained, while the hoax of illusory promises is rejected.

Yet the movement from aspiration to realization is enormously difficult and painful. Besides honesty and commitment, it demands courage—perhaps, we might even say, heroic courage. We have already seen at length, however, that the desire for heroism is very much alive today, and the evidence for this too is the Bomb, with its myth of heroic survival. Thus we need not find a heroism that doesn't yet exist, but only channel our desire for heroism in a new direction. And because the essence of the hero is a willingness to confront one's own death, it is clear that the Bomb has provided us with the basis for the new heroism as well. That is, the Bomb itself has given us the unalterable fact, for the last three decades, that each day—each moment—might be our last. The Bomb has imposed a constant threat of cataclysmic reversion to total chaos, the very threat that is the heart of the hero's experience.

If, then, we must confront our reality with full honesty, we must recognize that we have all been living the life of the mythic hero everyday. Like the heroic king of biblical times, we have walked through the valley of death. And we have feared no evil, for we have been numb. But in this numbing we find further evidence of our status as heroes, for psychic numbing is a "death in life." While we have been threatened by physical death, we have lived the reality of psychic death. All the "partial deaths" that mark modern culture are reflections of the "death in life" wrought by the Bomb, and all have forced us to be heroes whether we chose to be or not. If we escaped the numbing and faced our reality, we encountered yet a third form of the hero's trial: madness. We were forced to recognize that the craziness that surrounded us in the nuclear age was inevitably inside us as well, and so we were made to experience the reversion to psychic chaos that is part of every heroic myth.

Honesty compels us to admit, then, that we have been living in a classic ordeal, a classic test of initiation. We have had no choice; yet we may now turn this necessity into a virtue. For if our goal is to build and attain a new level on which to live, we must put ourselves into such an initiatory situation. Every transition to a new spiritual level demands the death of the old. For every higher level is a level of wider integration and greater wholeness, leaving behind a level of relative fragmentation. Thus we must allow ourselves to experience a dissolution of the parts of our lives, so that a new synthesis can be created. Certainly this must be true if wholeness is the meaning of the fourth level. And only in a direct confrontation with death can such a dissolution and merger be experienced. This is the evidence of religious traditions throughout the world. If we want to build a fourth level, we must accept and even embrace our initiatory experience as something positive. Of course we must also recognize that we have not completed the process; our three-decade initiatory chaos is still upon us, and only we ourselves can choose to complete the process. Nevertheless, we are en route, and it is the Bomb itself that has made this possible.

Our initiations must be in some sense individual and private, but they must also be done in community; society as a whole must undergo the experience. Hence we can learn our path not only from the myth of the individual hero but also from the myth of the heroic rebirth of whole peoples, even of the whole world. Indeed we have such a myth, kept alive for us by the Bomb, in the tradition of the apocalypse. We can learn something valuable from this tradition too. We can learn that our initiation must be acted out in real history—in the empirical reality of the political, social, and cultural world. And we can learn that no matter how bad things may be now, they must get worse before they get better. The chaos of today must be intensified; death must be given its full due before new life can begin.

We must face more honestly and more deeply the distortions in our lives—the insecurity of a fragmented and chaotic world whose survival hangs on such a slim thread. In doing so, we must admit that we feel ourselves living in desperate times and immersed to some degree or other in feelings of despair. Joanna Rogers Macy has written eloquently on this subject, showing how our numbing leads us to repress the despair that must arise from an honest assessment of our situation: "This refusal of feeling takes a heavy toll. . . . The energy expended in pushing down despair is diverted from more creative uses."[2] Macy suggests that we must allow ourselves to feel this despair if our life energy is to be freed again; this opening up of despair, as she describes it, clearly has initiatory dimensions. For in feeling the depth of our despair we may, in fact, "disintegrate." But this is "positive disintegration": "It is helpful in despair work to realize that going to pieces or falling apart is not such a bad thing. Indeed, it is as essential to evolutionary and psychic trans- formation as the cracking of outgrown shells. . . . Our 'going to pieces,' however uncomfortable a process, can open us up to new perception, new data, new response. . . . There is healing in such openness, for ourselves and perhaps for the world."[3] In admitting our craziness, we must face our despair. And in facing despair, we deepen our craziness. Yet it is a necessary part of our initiation.

We may also, temporarily, deepen our numbing. In any "positive disintegration" there is resistance, a natural refusal of the psyche to fall apart, and thus there is refusal to feel. But this, too, may have to be accepted as necessary, with trust that it is merely temporary and that those who accept the need to transcend their present state will transcend the numbing as well. Every facet of our "death in life" must be tasted to its fullest. In order to "imagine the real" we must open ourselves to the feelings of total craziness, total despair, and total numbing, as moments on our way to the fourth level.

This painful necessity points back to the central importance of symbolism. Macy writes: "To acknowledge and express our despair, we need images and symbols. . . . Exercise of the imagination is especially necessary, because existing verbal constructs seem inadequate to what many of us are sensing. . . . We are groping in the dark, with shattered beliefs and faltering hopes, and we need images for this phase if we are to work through it."[4] While the Bomb shows us once again our need for symbolic images, it also shows us that we may already have the images we need. For what better image of despair is there than the image of nuclear war itself? What better image of madness and of "death in life" than nuclear catastrophe? But the problem we have consistently encountered is the relatively unthreatening and even appealing elements in all these images. And it may be that all such images of chaos, expressing numinous power and the coincidence of opposites in the *big whoosh*, must inevitably have attractive aspects. Yet there may be some which come closer to reflecting the total horror of nuclear war. These are the images we must agree to face if we are to confront our despair and the reality that lurks behind it.

Where shall these images be found? Perhaps the best place to look for them is in Hiroshima, where the mythical terror became empirical reality. Not surprisingly, some survivors described their experience as a descent into hell: "The most impressive thing I saw was some girls, some very young girls, not only with their clothes torn off but with their skin peeled off as well. . . . My immediate thought was that this was like the hell I had always read about. . . . And I imagined that all of these people I was seeing were in hell. . . . I experienced such a dreadful event . . . and saw actual hell in this world."[5] There may be a certain fascination with images of hell, but they exercise less appeal than most other religious imagery, and they are perhaps the most appropriate analogue that the traditional religions have to the reality of nuclear war. Moreover, picturing ourselves in hell, whose punishment is usually imagined as eternal, we do not have the luxury of seeing ourselves as dead, obliterated in the *big whoosh*. Rather, we are condemned to unending suffering in a life that is neither truly life nor truly death. It is appropriate here to recall Schell's phrase, that nuclear war would mean the "death of death."[6] And, as the Hiroshima survivor said, hell would no longer be an alternative to life on earth—it would *be* life on earth. There would be no other realm available to us.

Along with this vision of hell, there was a perception in Hiroshima that people had been transformed into ghosts: "The appearance of people was . . . well, they all had skin blackened by burns. . . . They had no hair because their hair was burned, and at a glance you couldn't tell whether you were looking at them from in front or in back . . . . wherever I walked I met these people. . . . Many of them had died along the road—I can still picture them in my mind—like walking ghosts. . . . They didn't look like people of this world."[7] Lifton suggests an analogous image, found frequently in world folklore and mythology: "The homeless dead . . . condemned to a miserable transitional existence in which they are capable neither of rejoining the living nor of settling comfortably among the other dead (they are sometimes also called 'living dead')."[8] In a sense, of course, psychic numbing has already made all of us "living dead," but the image of the living dead has a special power when applied to a postnuclear-war world. As in the imagery of hell, there is little that is at all attractive. While many cultures affirm that the ghosts or homeless dead can be given a final resting place by the actions of living survivors (thereby making them "grateful dead"), after a nuclear war there would be no living survivors in the traditional sense; all would become wandering ghosts, unable to find a resting place to all eternity. Again, the "death of death" would make such a final rest impossible.

The mythic themes of hell and ghosts and the wandering dead are particularly appropriate here because, while they do speak of manifestations of power that may be sacred, they offer little in that power which is appealing. In fact, hell and the "nowhere land" of the homeless dead symbolize precisely what the Bomb takes away from us. The residents of these places have no power at all. They are in a place of total disorder, with no meaning to ease their minds. They cannot die and therefore do not have the comfort of transcending time. Their present suffering offers no hope of new or better life, and so they cannot rise to a new spiritual level. Nor do they have the luxury of feeling "unreal"; their pain and terror are too overwhelmingly real to be evaded. If the time comes when the Bomb delivers whatever it has to deliver, it seems likely that we shall discover not the positive side of its promise but only these negative aspects. Hence these images seem to be best suited to the task of "imagining the real."

As we look to the images of traditional religions for resources in this task, however, we must also remember that the "real" that we must imagine is in fact unprecedented in human history. No traditional religion has been called upon to reflect it in symbolic images. Thus we may also feel compelled to find new language to express this new reality. As Alvarez has suggested, there are those who can discover and develop such language; the true problem is getting people to listen to it. But the discovery of new language to meet a radically new situation is not easy. It will demand energetic exploration and experimentation on the part of many people, and it is impossible to predict what the results might be. In an age of extreme individualism, the most meaningful images may be those of isolation and alienation. Here, again, the symbolism of the Bomb itself may provide us with a place to start.

In discussing perceptions of the Bomb's effects, we saw that it may be impossible to picture a world with no survivors. We must project ourselves into the role of an imaginary survivor in order to relate to the phenomenon at all. Yet there may be greater terror in the idea of even a single survivor than in the thought of total annihilation, just because total annihilation cannot be a "thought." Given this situation, may we not "imagine the real" most effectively by projecting ourselves into the situation of the single survivor—the only survivor? As the only survivor, I would be compelled to experience the full degree of loss caused by nuclear war; nothing would exist except myself and my awareness of the otherwise complete annihilation. Of course, such a situation is hardly empirically likely; neither is the hell of traditional religions. Yet, to repeat, the aim here is to discover mythic images that allow us to "imagine the real" on the level of symbolic and psychological reality. And it may be that the myth of the lone survivor—a survivor who cannot in any way be heroic—projects us into the true psychic reality of nuclear war.

The isolation and terror of the lone survivor may not be totally beyond our ability to experience. In fact, each of us has had experiences that give us a glimpse of such a feeling. One such experience may have special relevance here, again an experience reflected in the symbolism of the Bomb itself. The Bomb creates a sense of unreality, as if we were living life in a dream, but with its dreadful shadow hanging over us, the dream becomes a nightmare. In our nightmares, we are alone. No one else shares the terror that we must face. And nuclear war would certainly be the ultimate nightmare; no matter how many others survived, each of us would have to live with the aloneness of a nightmare world. But we can go one step further.

On occasion, we wake up from a nightmare and feel the deep relief of returning to the normal world, only to find that world beginning to terrify us again. We are awake, and yet strange, surreal things are happening, things that usually occur only in nightmares. The strangeness grows and with it the terror, because now we are back in the "normal" world and yet we are being engulfed in nightmarish happenings. Finally the terror becomes unendurable. Then we awake, and we discover that the first "waking up" was only illusory—a part of the dream. May we not "imagine the real" of nuclear war most effectively by seeing it as the nightmare after the nightmare, the second nightmare, the one that takes place in the "real" world? But there is a crucial difference. In nuclear war, no matter how unendurable the terror, we can never "wake up," for we are already fully awake. We are as alone and as overwhelmed as in any nightmare, and yet we have nothing to look forward to but more of the same. If we fall asleep and dream a nightmare, we are condemned to wake up into a nightmare every time, with the terrible knowledge that we can never escape. The myth of "the nightmare from which no one ever awakes" may be an important one with which to confront the true reality of nuclear war.

The lone individual, isolated and alienated, is already an important motif in modern literature, of course, appearing most frequently as the hero, or more precisely the "antihero" of existentialist novels and drama. This character appears in situations in which decisions must be made, but no decision can yield a "heroic" outcome or make the character a hero. Perhaps the myth of the existential antihero is especially appropriate for imagining nuclear war. For it seems likely that in the face of an actual nuclear war, most of us will, from the very first warning signal, feel impelled to make decisions. The first decision may well be whether to stay where one is or try to reach another place. In deciding this question, however, a series of considerations will arise, each of which involves another set of decisions. Some of these may be of a more "practical" nature (Is there a safer place? Can I expect to reach it? Will there be food and shelter there?), while some will be value decisions (Who needs my help most? How much of my resources should I share with others, and with whom? What kinds of risks should I expose my children to?).

The factors involved in all these decisions will be tremendously complex, and they will have to be made all too quickly. For most of us, these will be the most agonizing decisions we have ever had to make and under the most unstable and emotionally taxing circumstances for decisionmaking that we have ever faced. Moreover, the circumstances are likely to be so chaotic that we shall have no way of gauging the results of our decisions; we shall know only that each decision will raise new demands for decisionmaking while simultaneously closing off potential options. Perhaps the most appropriate mythic image here is the darkness of the underground labyrinth, where we must choose our path at every junction with no sense of where any potential path might lead.

Of course, the chaos of full-scale nuclear war may render individual decisionmaking more or less irrelevant. Perhaps we shall be in such shock that we shall be swept away by a tide of events that we are both unable and unwilling to control. Perhaps we too shall perceive ourselves as dead, while still alive, and realize that the dead need make no decisions. Perhaps a short time in the darkness of the labyrinth will persuade us that decisionmaking is a cruel and useless hoax. So if one puts some image of decisionmaking at the center of the perception of nuclear war, one may well be creating a myth that will be incongruent with empirical reality. Yet such a myth would bring us closer to the realization that there will be nothing heroic about our decisionmaking process. For the actors in the drama of heroic initiation know that, like Theseus, they will emerge from the labyrinth triumphant and renewed, while existential antiheroes have no such assurance at all. They know, rather, that the outcome of all their decisionmaking is likely to be a life as full of pain and anxiety as that which they have now. Their world of chaos and dilemma is truly "hellish" because it has no end.

Clearly, no single image is the one "right" image for mirroring the psychological reality of nuclear war on the symbolic level. Some images will be more potent for some of us, and other images for others; for most of us, a combination of these images will be necessary. Perhaps part of our initiatory process, our movement to the fourth level, will be an exploration of a wide variety of such images, all of which will immerse us to some degree in the reality that we must confront. The crucial thing is that we do confront it, as fully and honestly as we can, while at the same time we also confront our existing "death in life," our despair, our refusal to deal honestly with our reality up until now.

This imaginative immersion in destruction, dissolution, and death is, however, only the first part of a two-part process. Every symbolic death must be followed by new life. So we must reap the fruits of our willingness to look squarely at nuclear death. Having accepted the task of transcending our limits through mythic imagination, and having seen the limitless chaos that surrounds us, we shall be able to see as well the limitless possibility that is opened up to us. A new world demands the dissolution of the old, but the corollary is that the dissolution of the old makes possible the birth of the new. And what is this new world? It is, quite simply, a world without nuclear weapons, a world in which we are trapped neither by the threat of physical destruction nor by the distortions of the technological death-God nor by the need to numb ourselves. If we can imagine the worst, we can also imagine the best. And here, too, the literal reality may elude us, leading us to look to the resources of myth. For myth affords the possiblity of experiencing this new world now, making it all the more likely that this new world will one day become a reality. Where will the appropriate myth for this final phase of our initiation be found?

Jonathan Schell writes: "Even by merely imagining for a moment that the nuclear peril has been lifted and human life has a sure foothold on the earth again, we can feel the beginnings of a boundless relief and calm—a boundless peace."[9] In the imagery of traditional religions, boundless peace can be found only in one place: paradise. Short of paradise, fulfillment can be imagined only as limited and partial. In paradise, as pictured in all the major religions, there is limitless harmony, tranquillity, and bliss. And the image of these can fill us with the same numinous awe that we now find only in nuclear weapons. Yet the awe comes not merely from the stupendous vision of unending life and peace, but from a life and peace that grow out of death and strife.

Once again, the symbolic meanings of the Bomb itself make such an experience possible for us. Schell says:

> If it is possible to speak of a benefit of the nuclear peril, it would be that it invites us to become more deeply aware of the miracle of birth, and of the world's renewal. "For unto us a child is born." This is indeed "good news." Yet when we turn from extinction, which silences us with its nothingness, to the abundance of life, we find ourselves tongue-tied again, this time by the fullness of what lies before our eyes. If death is one mystery, life is another, greater one. We find ourselves confronted with the essential openness, unfathomability, and indefinability of our species. . . . We can only feel awe before a mystery that both is what we are and surpasses our understanding.[10]

Schell speaks here on a more literal level of the birth of children in a nuclear-free world. Yet this literal fact is merely one part of the wider symbolic birth that would be brought about by the elimination of nuclear weapons. And Schell speaks of birth that is possible because death has been left behind. But on the symbolic level, as we have seen, the mystery is opened up to us only when we accept the necessary unity of life and death, a unity that is reflected in the myths of the emergence of paradise out of primal chaos.

Thus the myths of paradise speak of unlimited power that results in unlimited life because it has embodied and yet transcended unlimited death. They speak of unlimited order and structure, a perfection in which the elements of our world are synthesized without being dissolved, so that all conflict and discord is left behind. Surely they also speak of eternity and immortality, and they reflect a sense of unreality, the most wonderful dream imaginable. Paradise, in short, is the image of that wholeness to which we aspire; it embodies all of the symbolic meanings of the Bomb, and more. It goes on to fulfill the promise of a new and more positive life. Thus it can be a true image of that totally unlimited reality in which we wish to dwell.

It would be naïve to think that the elimination of nuclear weapons could, in itself, literally transform our world into paradise. Yet it would be equally naïve to think that the myth of paradise no longer exerts its fascination upon us. In the popular media, in advertising, in our leisure and recreational pursuits, all around us we find hints and reflections of a nostalgia for paradise that is still very much alive. Here, in the initiatory movement to the fourth level, this nostalgia may be evoked and put to a most constructive use. Without such a myth to complete our vision, the confrontation with death on the other three levels would be dismaying at best, and probably paralyzing. With such a myth, we can open our minds to the full reality of the situation, both at its worst and at its best. As with our images of destruction, so with our images of new creation we may have to draw on the resources of our religious past and add to them the discoveries and inventions of contemporary creativity. New languages and new myths of paradise may have to be found, but it seems quite certain that they can be found. Perhaps the world without the Bomb will itself become our most important new image of paradise.

Like every initiation, the movement toward the fourth level may best be pictured as a journey—a journey through the darkness into the light. If we choose to travel this path, we shall immerse ourselves in all those experiences that the Bomb now symbolizes. We shall feel the full intensity of both a Bomb*ed* and a Bomb*less* world and realize that both of these visions are necessary for "imagining the real." Darkness and light are complementary and equally essential moments of the whole journey—the journey toward wholeness.

On the journey to the fourth level we shall learn once again that life and death need each other. But we shall do more: we shall experience the intertwined powers of life and death directly. Facing these powers honestly, we shall absorb them into ourselves and make their unity our own. Our newfound personal power will be a limitless power, stemming as it does from a transcendence of limits, and it will enable us to stand up against the power of the Bomb. As we journey toward a world without threat, imagination infused with power will be unloosed in a myriad of creative and constructive ways. New symbols, new meanings, and new worldviews will arise to provide structure for a newly regained sense of transcendence.

A mythic journey of the imagination cannot replace awareness of the literal empirical facts. Nor can it replace political activity based on those facts. Empirical education, in which we learn to distinguish between true and false, and political action, in which we choose between right and wrong and find practical ways to implement our choices, will always be necessary. But as long as our awareness is merely literal and our activity merely political, we are confined to the realm of limited meanings and goals. Literalism and politics cannot lead us to the unity underlying the fragments of our experience. Symbolism and myth are the key to unification. They teach us to see better and worse as two sides of a single reality, even as they help us to struggle implacably against the worse in the name of the better. They transform our political struggle itself into an experience of wholeness. The means must suit the end. Perhaps the means are ultimately the same as the end. Only a synthesis of dark and light, unconscious and conscious, symbolic and literal, mythic and political, can offer the power of true wholeness.

This initiatory journey of mythicized politics and politicized myth is a sacred journey, as frightening as it is fascinating. But we need not make it alone. If we are to discover the power of transcendence within us, we can and must make our journey together, as did the religious communities of old. As Joanna Macy writes: "When we face the darkness of our time, openly and together, we tap deep reserves of strength within us. . . . In the synergy of sharing comes power."[11] No matter how many share it, however, the journey is sure to be long and arduous. It leads through vast unmapped territory, and we have no leaders or heroes to look to except ourselves. It may go on for 10,000 miles. But it starts with a single step. And every one of us, we may be surprised to learn, knows how to walk.

NOTES

Bibliographical data for the following citations appears in the bibliography.

Introduction
1. Glenn Gray, p. 20.

1. A Limitless Power
1. Lifton, *Broken Connection*, p. 370.
2. Shneidman, *Deaths of Man*, p. 188.
3. Otto, p. 14.
4. Ibid.
5. Fornari, p. 156.
6. Lifton, *Broken Connection*, p. 371.
7. Moss, p. 337.
8. Ibid., p. 24.
9. P. V. Chari quoted in Griffiths and Polanyi, p. 156.
10. Lifton, *Broken Connection*, p. 355.
11. Hillman, p. 86.
12. Otto, p. 26.
13. Lifton, *Death in Life*, pp. 305, 369.
14. Schell, p. 150.
15. Lifton, *Death in Life*, pp. 69, 72.
16. Ibid., p. 72.
17. Frank, p. 27.
18. Lifton, *Death in Life*, p. 80.
19. Carey, p. 23.
20. Fornari, p. 93.
21. Glenn Gray, p. 36.
22. Ibid.
23. Lifton, *Death in Life*, p. 26.
24. Lifton, *Broken Connection*, p. 350.
25. Caillois, pp. 164, 168, 175, 177.
26. Gray, p. 12.
27. Ibid., pp. 53, 56.
28. Lifton, *Death in Life*, p. 261.

29. Ibid., p. 27.
30. Ibid., p. 29.
31. Ibid., p. 79.
32. Lifton, *Broken Connection*, p. 371.
33. Ibid.
34. Schell, p. 147.
35. Anders, p. 292.
36. Lifton, *Broken Connection*, p. 346.
37. Hillman, p. 69.
38. Moss, p. 334.
39. Wald, p. 412.
40. Shneidman, *Deaths of Man*, pp. 184, 185, 194.
41. Mack, p. 19.
42. Cousins, p. 206.
43. Fussell, p. 71.
44. Lifton, *Death in Life*, p. 130.
45. Schell, pp. 95–96.
46. Gray, p. 216.
47. Alvarez, p. 112.
48. Anders, p. 288.
49. Ibid., p. 289.

2. The Many Meanings of "Security"

1. Moss, p. 109.
2. Ibid., p. 31.
3. Fussell, p. 76.
4. Gray, p. 132.
5. Moss, p. 241.
6. Lifton, *Broken Connection*, p. 353.
7. Katz, pp. 144–45.
8. Moss, p. 127.
9. Berger, p. 23.
10. Ibid., p. 24.
11. Ibid., p. 27.
12. Aho, p. 10.
13. Fussell, p. 79.
14. Ibid., p. 76.
15. Frank, p. 140.
16. Hart, p. 13.
17. Public Agenda, p. 18.
18. Lifton, *Broken Connection*, p. 373.

19. Schell, p. 197.
20. Ibid., p. 201.
21. Frank, pp. 143, 145.
22. *Time*, Sept. 26, 1983, p. 18.
23. Snow, p. 65.
24. Rowny, p. 70.
25. *Time*, March 29, 1982, p. 26.
26. Lifton, *Broken Connection*, p. 377.
27. Public Agenda, pp. 24, 36, 37.
28. Frank, p. 34.
29. *New York Times*, May 30, 1982, p. 1:1; June 4, 1982, p. 10:3.
30. Ellsberg, p. 4.
31. *Time*, Dec. 5, 1983, p. 44.

3. Fate and Chance

1. Snow, p. 59.
2. *Newsweek*, April 26, 1982, p. 24.
3. Shneidman, *Deaths of Man*, pp. 190–91.
4. Lifton, *Death in Life*, pp. 53–54.
5. Ibid., p. 21.
6. Ibid., p. 197.
7. Ibid., p. 369.
8. Shneidman, *Deaths of Man*, p. 191.
9. Moss, p. 39.
10. Schell, p. 29.
11. Griffiths and Polanyi, p. 39.
12. Schell, p. 32.
13. Cousins, p. 206.
14. Anders, p. 296.
15. Gray, p. 127.
16. Moss, p. 231.
17. Schell, p. 205.
18. Moss, p. 232.
19. Mack, p. 19.
20. Thompson, p. 91.
21. Lifton, *Death in Life*, p. 55.

4. Unreality and Madness

1. Carey, p. 21.
2. Fussell, p. 169.
3. Ibid., p. 170.
4. Alvarez, p. 217.

5. Lifton, *Death in Life*, p. 196.
6. Group for the Advancement of Psychiatry, p. 240.
7. Fornari, p. 157.
8. Schell, p. 117.
9. Fornari, pp. 123–24.
10. Ibid., p. 159.
11. Ibid., p. 160.
12. Carey, p. 22.
13. Lifton, *Death in Life*, p. 129.
14. Ibid., p. 500.
15. Schell, p. 143.
16. Fornari, p. 190.
17. Kahn, p. 26.
18. Ibid.
19. Schell, p. 195.
20. Moss, p. 206.
21. Lifton and Falk, p. 107.
22. Lifton, *Broken Connection*, p. 362.

5. Theater of the Absurd
1. Fussell, p. 191.
2. Ibid., p. 192.
3. Ibid.
4. Ibid., p. 221.
5. Ibid.
6. Marranca, p. 103.
7. Ibid.
8. Gray, p. 33.
9. Lifton and Falk, p. 51.
10. Marranca, p. 103.
11. Caillois, p. 155.
12. Aho, p. 31.
13. Smith, pp. 300–301.
14. Lifton, *Death in Life*, p. 25.
15. Fornari, p. 156.
16. Schell, p. 152.
17. Fornari, p. 185.
18. Chuang Tzu, p. 45.

6. The Myth of the Hero
1. Lifton, *Death in Life*, pp. 22–23.
2. Ibid., p. 97.

3. Ibid., pp. 481, 289, 110.
4. Lifton, *Broken Connection*, pp. 371–72.
5. Ibid., p. 369.
6. Shneidman, *Deaths of Man*, p. 192.

7. The Apocalyptic Vision
1. Defense Civil Preparedness Agency, p. iii.
2. Ibid., p. 3.
3. Ibid., p. 7.
4. Ibid., pp. 8–9.
5. Ibid., pp. 8, 33, 42.
6. Ibid., p. 27.
7. Ibid., p. 35.
8. Ibid., p. 39.
9. Ibid., p. iii.
10. Ibid., pp. 52–56.
11. Ibid., pp. 52–53.
12. Ibid., p. 15.
13. Scheer, pp. 18, 22.
14. Wald, p. 412.

8. Sacrifice and Martyrdom
1. Bhagavad-Gita, 10.32.
2. Ibid., 11.34.
3. Bourdillon, p. 41.
4. Quoted in Fornari, p. 23.
5. Ibid.
6. Gray, p. 45.
7. Meyer Fortes quoted in Bourdillon, p. xiv.
8. Ibid., p. xviii.
9. Fornari, p. 19.
10. Griffiths and Polanyi, p. 105.
11. Gray, p. 46.

9. Mutual Suicide
1. Stengel, pp. 58–59.
2. Stengel quoted in Shneidman, *Nature of Suicide*, p. 78.
3. Shneidman, *Nature of Suicide*, p. 118.
4. Lifton, *Broken Connection*, p. 249.
5. Ibid.
6. Shneidman, *Nature of Suicide*, pp. 15–16.

7. Lifton, *Broken Connection*, p. 251.
8. Shneidman, *Nature of Suicide*, p. 14.
9. Ibid., p. 40.
10. Ibid., p. 19.
11. Lifton, *Broken Connection*, p. 255.
12. Alvarez, p. 114.
13. Stengel, p. 130.
14. Sidney Jourard quoted in Shneidman, *Nature of Suicide*, p. 133.
15. Alvarez, p. 106.
16. Shneidman, *Nature of Suicide*, p. 133.
17. Lifton, *Death in Life*, p. 357.
18. Ibid., pp. 526, 387.
19. Alvarez, p. 45.
20. Lifton, *Death in Life*, pp. 207, 511.
21. Ibid., p. 533.
22. Alvarez, p. 94.
23. Shneidman, *Nature of Suicide*, p. 127.
24. Alvarez, p. 75.
25. Hillman, pp. 63, 91.
26. Quoted in Alvarez, p. 54.
27. Hillman, p. 62.
28. Ibid., pp. 63, 68.
29. Alvarez, p. 235.
30. Lifton, *Broken Connection*, p. 252.
31. Ibid.
32. Stengel, p. 116.
33. Ibid., p. 126.
34. Stengel quoted in Shneidman, *Nature of Suicide*, p. 78.
35. Stengel, p. 124.
36. Alvarez, p. 119.
37. Shneidman, *Nature of Suicide*, p. 120.
38. Ibid., p. 128.
39. Anders, pp. 291–92.
40. Alexander, p. 30.
41. Fried, Harris, and Murphy, p. 183.
42. Wald, p. 412.
43. Lifton, *Broken Connection*, p. 240.
44. Shneidman, *Nature of Suicide*, p. 36.
45. Hesse, p. 55.
46. Lifton and Falk, p. 77.

10. The Death-Machine as God

1. Group for the Advancement of Psychiatry, p. 234.
2. Moss, p. 129.
3. Lifton, *Broken Connection*, p. 22.
4. Ronze, p. 586.
5. Group for the Advancement of Psychiatry, p. 249.
6. Cousins, p. 158.
7. Fornari, p. 190.

Epilogue: Toward the Fourth Level

1. Lifton and Falk, p. 116.
2. Macy, p. 41.
3. Ibid., p. 43.
4. Ibid., p. 45.
5. Lifton, *Death in Life*, pp. 29, 372.
6. Schell, p. 119.
7. Lifton, *Death in Life*, p. 27.
8. Ibid., p. 492.
9. Schell, p. 172.
10. Ibid., p. 174.
11. Macy, p. 45.

BIBLIOGRAPHY

This bibliography includes all works cited in the text plus a selection of basic works that provide background on various subjects discussed in this book.

Aho, James A. *Religious Mythology and the Art of War.* Westport, Conn.: Greenwood Press, 1981.

Aldridge, Robert C. *First Strike! The Pentagon's Strategy for Nuclear War.* Boston: South End Press, 1983.

Alexander, Franz. "The Bomb and the Human Psyche." *United Nations World* 3, no. 11, November 1949.

Alvarez, A. *The Savage God: A Study of Suicide.* London: Weidenfeld & Nicolson, 1971.

Anders, Gunther. "Reflections on the H Bomb." In *Man Alone,* edited by Eric and Mary Josephson. New York: Dell Publishing Co., 1962.

Berger, Peter. *The Sacred Canopy.* Garden City, N.Y.: Doubleday & Co., 1967.

Bhagavad-Gita. Edited by F. Edgerton. Cambridge, Mass.: Harvard University Press, 1944.

Bourdillon, M. F. C., and M. Fortes, eds. *Sacrifice.* London: Academic Press, 1980.

Boyer, Paul. *By the Bomb's Early Light: American Thought and Culture at the Dawn of the Nuclear Age.* New York: Pantheon Books, 1985.

Buber, Martin. *I and Thou.* Translated by Walter Kaufmann. New York: Charles Scribner's Sons, 1970.

Caillois, Roger. *Man and the Sacred.* Translated by Meyer Barash. Glencoe, Ill.: Free Press, 1960.

Carey, Michael J. "Psychological Fallout." *Bulletin of the Atomic Scientists* 38, no. 1, January 1982.

Chapman, G. Clarke. *Facing the Nuclear Heresy.* Elgin, Ill.: Brethren Press, 1986.

Chuang Tzu. *Inner Chapters.* Translated by Gia-Fu Feng and Jane English. New York: Vintage Books, 1974.

Cohn, Norman. *The Pursuit of the Millennium.* Rev. ed. London: Oxford University Press, 1970.

Collins, John J. *The Apocalyptic Imagination in Ancient Judaism.* New York: Crossroads Publishing Co., 1984.

Coogan, Michael David. *Stories from Ancient Canaan.* Philadelphia: Westminster Press, 1978.

Cousins, Norman. *In Place of Folly.* New York: Washington Square Press, 1962.

Cross, Frank Moore. *Canaanite Myth and Hebrew Epic.* Cambridge, Mass.: Harvard University Press, 1973.

Davies, Nigel. *Human Sacrifice.* New York: Morrow, 1981.

Defense Civil Preparedness Agency. *Protection in the Nuclear Age,* 1977.

Dostoyevski, Fyodor. *Notes from Underground.* Translated by Mirra Ginsburg. New York: Bantam Books, 1982

Douglas, Mary. *Natural Symbols.* New York: Pantheon Books, 1970.

Edelstein, Ludwig. *The Meaning of Stoicism.* Cambridge, Mass.: Harvard University Press, 1966.

Eliade, Mircea. *Cosmos and History.* Translated by Willard R. Trask. New York: Harper & Row, 1959.

————. *Rites and Symbols of Initiation.* Translated by Willard R. Trask. New York: Harper & Row, 1965.

————. *The Two and the One.* Translated by J. M. Cohen. New York: Harper & Row, 1965.

Ellsberg, Daniel. "A Call to Mutiny." *Monthly Review* 33, no. 4, September 1981.

Ford, Daniel. *The Button: The Pentagon's Strategic Command and Control System.* New York: Simon & Schuster, 1985.

Fornari, Franco. *The Psychoanalysis of War.* Translated by Alenka Pfeifer. Bloomington: Indiana University Press, 1975.

Frank, Jerome D. *Sanity and Survival.* New York: Random House, 1967.

Fried, Morton; Marvin Harris; and Robert Murphy, eds. *War: The Anthropology of Armed Conflict and Aggression.* Garden City, N.Y.: Doubleday, Natural History Press, 1968.

Fussell, Paul. *The Great War and Modern Memory.* New York: Oxford University Press, 1975.

Gager, John G. *Kingdom and Community: The Social World of Early Christianity.* Englewood Cliffs, N.J.: Prentice-Hall, 1975.

Geertz, Clifford. *The Interpretation of Cultures.* New York: Basic Books, 1973.

Girard, René. *Violence and the Sacred.* Translated by Patrick Gregory. Baltimore: Johns Hopkins University Press, 1977.

Grant, Frederick C. *Hellenistic Religions.* Indianapolis, Ind.: Bobbs-Merrill, 1953.

Gray, J. Glenn. *The Warriors.* New York: Harper & Row, 1970.

Griffiths, Frank, and John C. Polanyi, eds. *The Dangers of Nuclear War.* Toronto: University of Toronto Press, 1979.

Group for the Advancement of Psychiatry. "Psychiatric Aspects of the Prevention of Nuclear War." Report No. 57. New York: Group for the Advancement of Psychiatry, 1964.

Hanson, Paul D. *The Dawn of Apocalyptic.* Rev. ed. Philadelphia: Fortress Press, 1979.

Hart, Gary, "A New Arms Control Agenda." Washington, D.C., 1982 (mimeograph).

Herken, Gregg. *Counsels of War.* New York: Alfred A. Knopf, 1985.

Hesse, Herman. *Steppenwolf.* Translated by Basil Creighton. New York: Bantam Books, 1969.

Hillman, James. *Suicide and the Soul.* New York: Harper Colophon Books, 1973.

Jewett, Robert. *The Captain America Complex.* 2nd ed. Santa Fe, N.Mex.: Bear & Co., 1984.

Kahn, Herman. *Thinking about the Unthinkable.* New York: Avon Books, 1966.

Kaplan, Fred. *The Wizards of Armaggedon.* New York: Simon & Schuster, 1983.

Katz, Arthur. *Life after Nuclear War: Economic and Social Consequences of Nuclear Attack on the United States.* Cambridge, Mass.: Ballinger Publishing Co., 1981.

Kennan, George F. *The Nuclear Delusion.* New York: Pantheon, 1982.

Kierkegaard, Søren A. *Fear and Trembling.* Translated by Walter Lowrie. Princeton, N.J.: Princeton University Press, 1941.

Koch, Klaus. *The Rediscovery of Apocalyptic.* London: SCM Press, 1972.

Koester, Helmut. *Introduction to the New Testament.* 2 vols. Philadelphia: Fortress Press, 1982.

Kurtz, Lester. *The Nuclear Cage.* Englewood Cliffs, N.J.: Prentice-Hall, 1986.

Lifton, Robert J. *The Broken Connection.* New York: Simon & Shuster, 1979.

———. *Death in Life: Survivors of Hiroshima.* New York: Random House, 1967.

Lifton, Robert J., and Richard Falk. *Indefensible Weapons.* New York: Basic Books, 1982.
Lifton, Robert J., and N. Humphrey. *In a Dark Time.* Cambridge, Mass.: Harvard University Press, 1984.
Linenthal, Edward T. *Changing Images of the Warrior Hero in America.* New York and Toronto: Edwin Mellen Press, 1982.
Mack, John E. "Psychosocial Effects of the Nuclear Arms Race." *Bulletin of the Atomic Scientists* 37, no. 4, April 1981.
Macy, Joanna Rogers. "How to Deal with Despair." *New Age Journal,* June 1979.
Marranca, Bonnie. "Nuclear Theater." *The Village Voice,* June 29, 1982.
McConeghey, Evelyn, and James McConnell, eds. *Nuclear Reactions.* Albuquerque, N. Mex.: Image Seminars, 1984.
Miller, Wayne Charles. *An Armed America: Its Face in Fiction.* New York: New York University Press, 1970.
Morgenthau, Hans J. "Death in the Nuclear Age." *Advances in Thanatology* 4, no. 2, 1980.
Moss, Norman. *Men Who Play God.* New York: Harper & Row, 1968.
Nillson, Martin P. *A History of Greek Religions.* 2nd ed. Oxford: Clarendon Press, 1963.
Otto, Rudolf. *The Ideea of the Holy.* Translated by J. W. Harvey. London: Oxford University Press, 1958.
Perrin, Norman, and Dennis C. Duling. *The New Testament: An Introduction.* 2nd ed. New York: Harcourt Brace Jovanovich, 1982.
Peters, F. E. *The Harvest of Hellenism.* New York: Simon & Schuster, 1971.
Pettazzoni, Raffaele. *The All-Knowing God.* Translated by H. J. Rose. London: Methuen Press, 1956.
Powers, Thomas. *Thinking about the Next War.* New York: Alfred A. Knopf, 1982.
Pringle, Peter, and William Arkin. *SIOP: The Secret U.S. Plan for Nuclear War.* New York: W. W. Norton, 1983.
The Public Agenda Foundation, in collaboration with the Center for Foreign Policy Development at Brown University. *Voter Options on Nuclear Arms Policy.* New York: The Public Agenda Foundation, 1984.
Reynolds, Frank E., and Earle H. Waugh, eds. *Religious Encounters with Death.* University Park: Pennsylvania State University Press, 1977.

Ringgren, Helmer. *Israelite Religion.* Translated by David E. Green. Philadelphia: Fortress Press, 1966.

Rist, John M. *Stoic Philosophy.* Cambridge, England: Cambridge University Press, 1969.

Ronze, Bernard. "La Mort Collective." *Etudes* 351, no. 6, December 1979.

Rowny, Edward L. "How Not to Negotiate with the Russians." *Reader's Digest,* June 1981.

Russell, Bertrand. *Has Man a Future?* Harmondsworth, England: Penguin Books, 1961.

Russell, D. S. *The Method and Message of Jewish Apocalyptic.* Philadelphia: Westminster Press, 1964.

Scheer, Robert. *With Enough Shovels.* New York: Random House, 1982.

Schell, Jonathan. *The Fate of the Earth.* New York: Avon Books, 1982.

Selg, Herbert, ed. *The Making of Human Aggression.* New York: St. Martin's Press, 1975.

Shneidman, Edwin S. *Deaths of Man.* New York: Quadrangle Books, 1973.

Shneidman, Edwin S., ed. *On the Nature of Suicide.* San Francisco: Josey Bass, 1973.

Smith, Jonathan Z. *Map Is Not Territory.* Leiden: E. J. Brill, 1978.

Snow, Donald M. *Nuclear Strategy in a Dynamic World.* University, Ala.: University of Alabama Press, 1981.

Stengel, Erwin. *Suicide and Attempted Suicide.* Baltimore: Penguin Books, 1964.

Thompson, E. P. "A Letter to America." *The Nation* 232, no. 3, January 24, 1981.

Tillich, Paul. *Dynamics of Faith.* New York: Harper & Row, 1957.

———. *The Protestant Era.* Translated by J. L. Adams. Chicago: University of Chicago Press, 1948.

———. *The Theology of Culture.* New York: Oxford University Press, 1959.

Turner, Victor. *Dramas, Fields, and Metaphors.* Ithaca, N.Y.: Cornell University Press, 1974.

———. *The Ritual Process.* Chicago: Aldine Publishing Co., 1969.

Van der Leeuw, Gerardus. *Religion in Essence and Manifestation.* Translated by J. E. Turner. 2 vols. New York: Harper & Row, 1963.

Wald, George. "A Generation in Search of a Future." *Vital Speeches* 35 (April 15, 1969): 412.

White, Ralph K. *Fearful Warriors: A Psychological Profile of U.S.–Soviet Relations.* New York: Free Press, 1984.

Winter, Gibson, "Hope for the Earth: A Hermeneutic of Nuclearism." *Religion and Intellectual Life* 1, no. 3, Spring 1984.

Yankelovich, Daniel. "Doomsday Logic and the Draft." *Psychology Today* 16, no. 3, March 1982.

INDEX

Abraham, 115, 116.
Absurdity: of Bomb, 66–68, 116; chance as, 59; faith as, 116; in modern life, 130; of rationality, 74. *See also* Humor of the absurd, Chance.
Aho, James, 37–38, 79.
Alexander, Franz, 129–130.
Alvarez, A., 64, 122, 124, 125.
Ambivalence: acted out in play, 81; in religious experience, 21, 36, 84; toward Bomb, 59, 81, 116, 141; toward chance, 60–61; toward madness, 73; toward suicide, 120, 121; toward theater and dreams, 83; toward omnipotence, 100; toward ourselves, 31.
Anders, Gunther, 27, 31, 57, 128.
Annihilation: in apocalypticism, 92; appeal of, 23, 25, 29–30, 129; Bomb protects against, 40–41; Bomb as symbol of, 13; of enemy as goal, 34; fear of, 35; Hiroshima survivor's wish for, 123; ignored in Civil Defense myth, 104; as inescapable, 17, 55; noncombatants as objects of, 33; and omnipotence, 30; and rebirth, 85–88; sacrifice as defense against, 111; as spectacle, 76; threat of, and ritual, 51; unreality of, 64.
Anomie, 36–37, 46, 51–52, 129, 131.
Apocalypticism: appeal of, 97–99; battle against nature as, 139; characteristics of, 91–92; in Christianity, 95–97; as cleansing, 110; evil in, 143; historical influence of, 98; and literalism, 153; martyrdom and, 117; and mechanization, 139; in nuclear age, 97–99; not applicable in nuclear age, 99–100; sacrifice and, 115; value of, 159.

Arms control, 43–44.
Atom, 15, 99, 107.
Atomic scientists. *See* Scientists, Experts.
Awe: of Bomb, 12–14, 19; of experts (*see also* Experts), 51, 70; experts' avoidance of, 69; of paradise, 166; toward reasoning, 72; in religious experience, 12–13; of war, 23.

Berger, Peter, 36–37.
Bible, 25, 109.
Bhagavad-Gita, 107.
Big bang, 26, 87. *See also* Creation.
Big whoosh: appeal of, 31, 131–132; as end of time, 26; nuclear war as, 23, 130; as sacrifice, 108; as suicide, 131. *See also* Annihilation.
Bouthoul, Gaston, 109.
"Brinkmanship," 60.
Buber, Martin, 151.

Canaanite religion, 93–94, 98.
Caillois, Roger, 23.
Captain America myth, 89.
Chance, 59–62, 77, 127–128. *See also* Absurdity, Uncertainty.
Chaos: alternative worldviews as, 40; Bomb as symbol of, 47; in Canaanite and Israelite religion, 93–94; as enemy, 142; modern life as, 130; nuclear blast as, 23; nuclear age as, 158, 164; nuclear war as, 31; preexisting, in Bible, 25; return to, as rebirth, 85; ritual and, 50, 51; and suicide, 131; threat of, 37; timelessness of, 26.
Christianity, 91, 95–97, 117, 120.
Churchill, Winston, 41.
Civil defense, 101–105.

182

Cognitive dissonance, 93, 94, 95, 96, 97.
Coincidence of opposites, 7, 25, 37, 46, 144. *See also* Unity.
Cold War, 4, 34, 45, 77.
Cold warrior, 37–38.
Comedy. *See* Humor of the absurd.
Contradiction, 6–7, 39, 46–47, 120, 148.
Cousins, Norman, 28.
Craziness. *See* Madness.
Creation: as birth, 85 (*see also* Rebirth); preceded by destruction, 85–86 (*see also* Initiation); nuclear explosion as, 26, 86; myth of, 25; nuclear power as, 15–16; by otiose God, 18.
"Creature-feeling," 30, 53, 57.

da Vinci, Leonardo, 131.
Death: acceptance of, 28, 39; Bomb as protection against, 59; Bomb as symbol of all, 68; causeless, 27; control over, in suicide, 131; desired by survivors, 124; divinized, 24, 143, 146–147; as enemy, 93, 142; fear of, 128; fatalism and, 58; as ideal, 146; inability to conceive of, 64; inescapable, 17; Krishna as, 107; and life experienced together, 167; mass appeal of, 65; meaningfulness of, 58–59, 66; reality of, denied in suicide, 122; as religious concern, 84–85; revelation of God and, 18; sacrifice as control of, 110–111 (*see also* Sacrifice); symbolic, of hero, 88; as total annihilation, 68; value of, 24; and wisdom, 16.
"Death in life": aspiration to, 146; as initiatory, 158; loss of order and, 25; in modern culture, 121; as psychosis, 67; and suicide, 121.
The Deer Hunter, 138.
Defense intellectuals. *See* Strategists, Experts.
Deus otiosus, 18.

Devil, 36, 110.
Defense Civil Preparedness Agency, 101.
Deterrence, 42–44, 59–60, 77.
Diamond, Stanley, 130.
Disarmament movement, 39–40, 51, 154–155.
Disorder. *See* Chaos.
Dr. Strangelove, 23, 53.
Drama. *See* Theater, Ritual.
Dream, 81–83. *See also* Nightmare.
Durkheim, Emile, 109, 129.
Dualism, 33–36, 39, 92.
Dual track, 43–48.

Ecstasy, 19, 23.
Einstein, Albert, 55, 61.
Eliade, Mircea, 25.
Ellsberg, Daniel, 49.
Enemy: as absolute, 33; as abstraction, 33; disorder as, 37–38, 44, 142 (*see also* Chaos); death as, 142; defeat of, 46; depiction of, in world wars, 38; fantasies of, in MAD, 42; fear of, 32; instant destruction of, 36; irrationality as, 47; as omnipotent, 34; responsible for all evil, 35; as sacred, 110; sacrifice of, 109–110, 114; in suicide, 123, 125; threat of nuclear war against, 49; threatens freedom, 34. *See also* Dualism.
The Enlightenment, 45, 154–155.
Eternity: Bomb as a symbol of, 27–29; of cosmic structure, 44; desire for, 118, 128, 157; effects of war and, 29; hell as, 160; moment of creation as, 26; in myth of heroic survivors, 88; nuclear explosion as, 26; nuclear war and, 27, 29; safety of, through MAD, 42; of worldview, 37, 39. *See also* Time, Transcendence.
Experts, 50–51, 52, 58, 69–72. *See also* Strategists, Scientists.
Explosion, 12, 19, 21, 24, 60.
Extinction, 27, 130–131. *See also* Annihilation.

Fantasy: appeal of living out, 83; falsified by information, 152; monopolized by government, 68; nuclear fears as, 13–14; and nuclear war, 87; of omnipotence, 30, 45, 82; and reality merge, 153; in suicide, 124, 125, 127; of survival, 66; war as, 115.

Fascination: of annihilation, 25, 29–30, 132; of Bomb, 19, 86; of death and disorder, 143; of myth, 89; of numinous, 19; of paradise myths, 167; of unreality, 80; of war, 23, 24, 76.

Fascism, 97.

Fatalism: in apocalypticism, 92; "creature feeling" in, 57; makes death meaningful, 58–59; of Hiroshima survivors, 54; early 1960s and, 53; and optimism, 59; and pessimism, 59; and stoicism, 58; and transcendence of time, 58.

Fate, 56–59, 127–128.

Fear: absence of, 28; of chance, 61; defense against, 48; of enemy, 32, 38; of extinction, 128–129; of future, 27–28; intensified in modernity, 143; heroic survivors' lack of, 88; of nuclear destruction, 14; prevents new responses, 55; in public opinion, 54; of self, 140.

Film, 17, 23, 53, 76, 98, 138.

First strike, 48, 49.

Fornari, Franco, 13, 21, 22, 65, 68.

Frank, Jerome D., 18.

Freedom: and anomie, 51; defense of, as ritual, 49; limited by enemy, 34–35; nation as symbol of, 34; as omnipotence, 46 (see also Omnipotence); and security in ritual, 51; suicide and, 125, 127, 131.

Fussel, Paul, 29, 33, 64, 75, 76.

Future, 27–28, 121.

Gamble, 60–61, 127. See also Chance, Uncertainty.

Games, 78–80. See also Play.

Garwin, Richard, 114.

Ghosts, 161.

Gift, 106–108.

Girard, René, 112–113.

God: acts in politics, 99; in apocalypticism, 91–95 (see also Apocalypticism); attributes of, 17; Bomb as, 63, 133, 136–142; as creator, 15, 106; death as, 146–147; as source of death, 147; in deism, 45; as destroyer, 36, 107; devil as creature of, 36; ends time, 26; experience of, 8; fear of, 15; fellowship with, 109–110; hidden, 18; history as manifestation of, 58; control of history, 91–92, 99–100; humans as, 100; initiation of, 22; justice of, 38, 127; love of, 41; as machine, 136–138 (see also Machine); merger with, 51; nation as, 9; omnipotence of, 93, 94; as redeemer, 97, 142; needs sacrifice, 106–107; and suicide, 127, 131; as truth, 16; as warrior, 94; wisdom of, 45, 92; works instantly, 26, 36.

Government: decisions left to, 55–57; denies change, 68; uses experts' language, 72; limits freedom, 35; madness and, 68; belief in omnipotence, 30; possesses atomic secret, 58; power reinforced by military spending, 112; powerlessness of, 55–56, 69; represses anxiety, 48; skepticism about survival in, 104–105; suicidal thinking of, 122; supports heroic survivors myth, 101; theatricalism of, 76; sense of unreality in, 68–69; urges rationality, 50–51. See also Leaders.

Gray, J. Glenn, 3, 22, 23, 24, 58, 76, 110.

Guilt: absence of, 68, 140; fantasies generate, 66; scientists don't feel, 16; suicide and, 124; survival and, 61–62.

Hell, 160–161, 165.
Hellenistic culture, 56, 58, 59, 126.
Helplessness, 55–58, 64, 89. *See also*
Powerlessness.
Hero: as automaton, 137; desire for,
157; everyone as, 157; impossibility
of, in nuclear war, 163; initiatory rebirth of, 88 (*see also* Initiation);
myth of, 88–89, 100; myth of, and
suicide, 127.
Heroic survival: and apocalypticism,
97; belief in, 116; myth of, 87–90;
myth of, in science fiction, 87–90;
myth of, supported by government,
101, 104; relocation as, 103.
Hesse, Herman, 131.
Hibakusha. See Hiroshima survivors.
Hillman, James, 16, 27, 125, 126.
Hiroshima survivors: craziness and,
67; experienced rebirth, 86; experienced descent into hell, 160; fatalism of, 54, 61; feeling of world dying, 86; feelings of helplessness, 54;
as ghosts, 161; guilt feelings of, 124;
loss of self among, 23; loss of structure, 24–25; nightmarish experience
of, 81; sense of contagion, 18; sense
of ineffability, 17, 63–64; wish for
nuclear war, 123.
History: child sacrifice in, 115; end of,
27; mythic interpretation of, 98–99;
of nuclear symbolism, 134; plan of,
58, 91; terror of, 28; war in, 38. *See
also* Time.
Hostages, 43, 47.
Humor of the absurd, 78, 80.

"I–Thou," 151, 155.
Identity, 8, 24, 138. *See also* Self.
Immortality, 111, 117, 128–129, 138.
See also Eternity.
Immutability, 42–44, 46.
Impersonality, 108, 137, 138.
Ineffability, 17, 56, 63–64.
Infinite power. *See* Limitless power.
Initiation: despair and, 159; of gods,

Initiation (*continued*):
93–94; of heroic survivors, 88–90;
as journey, 167; nuclear age as, 158;
as ritual rebirth, 85; shelters as huts
for, 102; war as, 24. *See also* Rebirth.
Insecurity, 35, 47–48, 51–52, 129–
130. *See also* Security.
Invulnerability, 33, 35, 42, 50, 111.
Iron Curtain, 50.
Irrationality, 41, 43, 46, 59–60, 74.
Israel, 93–94.

Japan, 30. *See also* Hiroshima survivors.
Jesus, 95.

Kahn, Herman, 69–71.
Kennedy, John F., 55.
Kierkegaard, Søren, 115–116.
Krishna, 107.

Labyrinth, 147, 164.
Language: of arms race, 113; of experts, 55, 69–72; new, difficulty of
finding, 63–64; new, denial of, 64;
new, need for, 160, 162; and psychic numbing, 71–72.
Laurence, William, 26, 41, 86.
Leaders (political and military): contradictions of, 46; as hostages, 47;
feeling of impotence, 55–56; as
parts of nuclear machine, 137; rationality of, 60, 119; suicidal behavior
of, 120; values of, 155.
See also Government.
Lifton, Robert, 17, 18, 23, 25, 29, 35,
64, 124, 138, 152, 161; concept of
death-in-life, 121, 135–136; concept
of survivor mentality, 123; on secrecy, 16; study of nuclear scientists,
86; theory of psychic numbing, 67,
128; theory of suicide, 121–122.
Limitless power: in apocalypticism, 94;
of Bomb, 14; and chance, 61; disarmament as, 167; dual track as, 44;

Limitless power (*continued*):
experts' control of, 51; and release from structure, 22; in religious experience, 13; as salvation, 46; secret of, 16; as solution to all problems, 31; union with through self-sacrifice, 117–118; in war, 23. *See also* Omnipotence.
Literalism: in disarmament movement, 154–155; of experts, 72, 74; effects of, 153–155; inadequate for nuclear war, 13, 152–153; limits of, 168; strengthens nuclear symbols, 154; value of, 156, 168.

MacArthur, Douglas, 40, 49.
Machine: Bomb as, 136–140; and desire for risk, 138; and desire for domination, 139; human beings as, 137–140; as meaningless, 145; as omnipotent, 136; and progress, 142; as weapon, 143; world as, 138. *See also* Technology.
Macy, Joanna Rogers, 159–160, 168.
MAD (Mutually Assured Destruction): appeal of, 42; and chance, 59, 77; irrationality of, 48; origin of, 41; seen as rational, 60; stresses symbolic meanings, 41–42; suicide and, 120.
Madness: alternative worldviews as, 40; as escape, 73; and experts' language, 72; fear of, 66; and humor, 78; as initiatory, 158; and myth, 80; of nuclear weapons, 66; in religion, 63; of self and Bomb merge, 77; and suicide, 120; survivors of Hiroshima and, 67; threat of annihilation and, 68.
Mailer, Norman, 27.
Marranca, Bonnie, 76, 77.
Martyrs, 117–118, 126.
Massive retaliation, 41, 48.
McMahon, Brien, 33.
Meal, 109.
Metaphors, 74–75.

"Missile gap," 56.
Money, 109, 112.
Monotheism, 36. *See also* God, Unity.
Moss, Norman, 14, 15, 70.
"Mutual suicide," 119, 120, 128.
Mystery: of atom, 15–16; of Bomb, 16–17; experts' command of, 70; fascination of, 19; in religious experience, 14; and rationality blend, 51. *See also* Secret.
Myth: as abstraction, 80; apocalypticism and, 93–94; of civil defense, 100–105; of heroic survivors, 87–90; historicizing of, 98–99; humor in, 80–81; response to Bomb as, 86–87; and theater, 89.

Nagasaki, 27, 81.
Nationalism, 9, 97, 103, 145.
National security, 32, 39, 40.
Nightmare, 14, 81–82, 122, 163. *See also* Dream.
Nomos: Bomb protects, 39, 42; makes death meaningful, 39; meaning of, 36; reliance on, 48; sacralized, 37; security of, 40; universal, as goal, 45; war as preservation of, 37. *See also* Worldview.
Numbing. *See* Psychic numbing.
Numinous: concept of, 12–13; desire for, 157; experts as, 51, 70; fascination of, 19; and fatalism, 57; humanity as, 31; mystery in, 14–15; nuclear blast as, 13–15; as stupor, 16. *See also* Awe.

Omnipotence: Bomb as symbol of, 15, 31; divine, 36, 58, 93 (*see also* God); enemy frustrates, 34–35; fantasy of, 82; and fatalism, 55; freedom as, 34, 46; of human beings, 30–31, 100; limits on, 34; and mystery, 15; and suicide, 125, 128. *See also* Limitless power.
Omnipresence, 17–18, 125, 147.
Omniscience, 17. *See also* Wisdom.

On the Beach, 17, 53.
Oppenheimer, Robert, 107.
Opposites. *See* Coincidence of opposites, Dualism.
Optimism, 57, 59.
Order: Bomb as symbol of, 47; cold war as maintenance of, 37–38; eternal, in apocalypticism, 94; fatalism and, 58; as goal of suicide, 127; natural, lost in nuclear blast, 25; natural and social, linked, 94; ritual and, 50–51; war reestablishes, 37–38. *See also* Structure.
Otto, Rudolph, 12, 21, 30.

Paradise, 165–167.
Paradox, 8, 108, 129. *See also* Contradiction.
Peace: as goal, 45; from imagining disarmament, 165; nuclear weapons as means to, 41, 43–46; and sacrifice, 113; sacrifice of, 39; war as prelude to, 94; and war merge, 44.
Pessimism, 59, 90.
Play: acceptance of ambivalence in, 81; appeal of, in religion, 80–81; as end in itself, 80; indistinguishable from real life, 79; nuclear theater as, 78–79; nuclear war as, 74–75; as ritual, 79. *See also* Games.
Potlach, 112.
Power: appeal of, in war, 76; Bomb as single, 17, 47; of creation, 15; of dreams, 83; of Enemy as sacred, 110; fascination of, 20; human relation with, 20; humans share Bomb's, 57, 108; in religious experience, 13; sacrifice as means to, 107; of sacrificial victim, 109; scientists possess, 15; suicide as means to, 126–127. *See also* Limitless power, Omnipotence.
Powerlessness: appeal of, 140; and depression, 56; experts foster, 70; government and, 69; of Hiroshima survivors, 18; and mechanization, 138;

Powerlessness (*continued*):
and modern age, 56; religious meaning of, 57–58; and social change, 96; and suicide, 120, 124–125; worship of, 56–57. *See also* Helplessness.
President, 55, 97.
Progress, 50, 57, 142.
Projection, 48, 125, 143–144, 154.
Psychic numbing: appeal of, 146; as avoidance of madness, 67; Bomb as cure for, 141; and boredom, 61; deepened in initiation, 159; dreaming and, 82; of experts, 70; and guilt, 124; honesty as escape from, 150; information counteracts, 152; intolerable, 141; limits of theory of, 135–136; and literalism, 153–154; and materialism, 139; and mechanization of life, 137–138, 140; nuclear weapons intensify, 137–138; prevents faith, 116; and symbolism of Bomb, 135–136; symbolism as escape from, 141; and symbolic immortality, 67; and suicide, 121; and theater, 78.
Public opinion, 40, 46, 54.
Pynchon, Thomas, 76.

Randomness. *See* Chance.
Rationality: in disarmament movement, 155; of experts, 49, 69–71; and MAD, 60; and mystery blend, 52; as source of order, 45; of suicide, 122, 126; in war planning, 60.
Rebirth: in apocalypticism, 92; desire for, 157; disarmament as, 165–168; flight to wilderness as, 103; of Hiroshima survivors, 86; in myth, 88, 94; nuclear war as, 102–104; nuclear suicide as, 127. *See also* Hero, Initiation.
Redemption. *See* Salvation.
Relocation plans, 103.
Renewal, 27, 110. *See also* Rebirth.
Repression: of anxiety by government,

Repression (*continued*):
48; of despair, 159; of desire for release, 22; of fascination with death,
143–144; of insecurity, 47–48; literalism as, 154; psychic numbing and,
68; and return of repressed, 143.
See also Unconscious.
Risk. *See* Chance, Uncertainty.
Ritual: as abstraction, 80; death as, in
sacrifice, 110–111; destruction as,
112; goal of, 51; nuclear, 49–50; as
play, 79–80; as release from structure, 22; as repetition of creation,
25; sacrifice as, 106; suicide as, 124,
127; war as, 79.
Rowny, Edward L., 43.
Russell, Richard, 105.

Sacrifice: of child, 115–116; definition
of, 106; desire for immortality in,
111, 117; desire for power in, 107;
desire for union in, 108; as discharge of social violence, 113; facing
death through, 126; as gift, 106–
109; human, 114–118; military
spending as, 112; nuclear war as,
107; resolves social conflict, 113; of
self, 117–118; social functions of,
111–113; as structured death, 110–
111; as theater, 113; of values, 34;
vicarious, 108–109; war as, 24.
Safety. *See* Security, Invulnerability.
Salvation: Christian concept of, 95; effortless, 50; nature of, 19; through
nuclear weapons, 39, 46; war as, 38.
Schell, Jonathan, 27, 29, 41, 68, 82,
160, 165–166.
Scientists, 15, 16, 102. *See also* Experts.
Science fiction, 87–88, 122.
Secret, 15–16, 47, 57, 70, 92. *See also*
Mystery.
Security: in apocalypticism, 92; desire
for, creates insecurity, 47, 140; and
freedom in ritual, 51; in MAD, 42;
meaning of, 40, 46; order and disor-

Security (*continued*):
der in, 36–37, 46–47; sacrifice as
means of, 111; traditional concept
reasserted, 48–49; worldview gives,
39–40. *See also* Invulnerability, National security.
Self: detachment from, in war, 75; as
dilemma, 31; loss of, 23, 77; as machine, 140; release from, 22; sacrifice of, in war, 117; subordination
of, in war, 23; suicide as affirmation
of, 125; suicide gives structure to,
127. *See also* Identity.
Seneca, 126.
Sexuality, 20–22, 28.
Shelter, 42, 102.
Shneidman, Edwin S., 53, 125.
Smith, Jonathan Z., 80, 81.
Snow, Donald M., 43.
Soldier. *See* Warrior.
Soviet Union: concern for, in U.S., 45;
Christianity in, 91; as evil, 33; fear
of, 46; intransigence of, 44; as ini-
tiator of nuclear war, 44; as protec-
tion against anomie, 50; nuclear ar-
mament in, 10; nuclear capacity of,
35; as symbol of instability, 44; U.S.
nuclear armament and, 48.
Spectacle, 76–77, 79. *See also* The-
ater.
Stability, 44–45. *See also* Order,
Structure.
Star Wars, 98.
Stengel, Erwin, 120, 127.
Stimson, Henry, 46.
Stoicism, 58.
Stranger, 89, 114.
Strategic Defense Initiative, 134.
Strategists: assumptions of, 71; foster
unreality, 69–72; language of, 55
(*see also* Language); suicide and
thinking of, 122; values of, 155. *See
also* Experts.
Structure: abolished in nuclear blast,
23; breakdown of, 96 (*see also* Cha-
os); in deism, 45; desire for, in mo-

Structure (*continued*):
dernity, 97–98; through nationalism, 51 (*see also* Nationalism); need for, 21; rejection of, 60; release from, 22, 25; social burden of, 113. *See also* Order.

Suicide: as affirmation of life, 125; as attempt at renewal, 27; as assertion of independence, 125–126; as cry for help, 123; desire for chaos in, 131; desire for immortality in, 128–129; desire for structure in, 127; as escape from anomie, 129–130; as escape from fate, 126; as expression of anger, 123; as gamble, 127–128; guilt and, 124; and hopelessness, 120; and madness, 120; nuclear war as, 41, 105; as quest for power, 126–127; partial, 121; as revenge, 125; as spiritual trial, 127; tendencies heightened by Bomb, 120–122, 129; as vitalizing act, 128.

Superpowers, 10, 34, 77, 137.

Survival: assumed in nuclear war myths, 90; belief in, 65; Bomb guarantees, 41; consolation of, 65; fear of, 65; guilt and, 61–62; myth of, in Civil Defense pamphlet, 101–104.

Survivor: anger of, 123–124; guilt feelings of, 124; as homeless dead, 161; lack of freedom of, 35; only, image of, 162; rebirth implied, 86; as subhuman, 90. *See also* Hiroshima survivors.

Symbolic immortality, 67.

Technology: absurdity of, 74; and control, 111; and death, 146; and destruction, 142; denies meaning, 145; effects of, 144–145; as experience of power, 20; fosters psychic numbing, 70; and heroic survival, 89; knowledge and, 151; and literalism, 153; and omnipotence, 82; and powerlessness, 56; as progress, 50; ratio-

Technology (*continued*):
nality of, 45; spiritual meaning of, 138. *See also* Machine.

Tertullian, 116.

Theater, 75–79, 89, 140. *See also* Spectacle, Play.

Thompson, E. P., 61.

Tillich, Paul, 13, 144–145.

Time, 25–27, 42, 44, 128. *See also* Eternity, History.

Timelessness. *See* Eternity.

Totem, 109.

Transcendence: as coincidence of opposites, 25; in counterculture, 28; desire for, 22, 84–85; disarmament and, 167–168; explosion as, 21; fatalism as, 59; of ignorance, 57; through imagination, 165; in modernity, 22; nuclear war as, 31, 131–132; of time, 26, 42, 44 (*see also* Eternity); of understanding, 14.

Trench warfare: fatalism in, 58; language for, 64; in MAD, 43; permanence of, 28, 76; psychology of, 33.

Turner, Victor, 22, 113.

Uncertainty, 59–61, 77, 138. *See also* Chance.

Unconscious: alienation from, 68, 154; anxieties, 13, 47; desire for heroic rebirth, 88; desire for war, 115; survival fantasies, 66; symbols as, 8, 134; war images, 82. *See also* Repression.

Unity: of all nuclear weapons, 17, 47, 55, 137; Bomb as symbol of, 147; with Bomb's power, 117–118; desire for, 147, 157; disarmament and, 167–168; in dual track, 46–47; with God in sacrifice, 108–109; of gods and devils, 110; of life and death, 166; loss of, 150; of nuclear symbolism, 52; nuclear war as means to, 132; prevented by technology, 145; regaining, 151; in religious experience, 20; of society in sacrifice and

Unity (*continued*):
war, 109–110; symbols express, 168; symbols of, repressed, 144. *See also* Coincidence of opposites.

Unreality: of alternative worldviews, 40; appeal of, 74; of Bomb, 66; myth as, 87; in nuclear age, 122; of nuclear war, 70, 78–79; of nuclear weapons, 89; sense of, in government, 68; strategic theories create, 69–70; of suicide, 124; in war, 75, 80–81.

van der Leeuw, Gerardus, 13.
Vitality: death experience evokes, 126; desire for, in modern life, 20; loss of, 121, 124, 126, 138, 146; suicide as quest for, 128; in war, 30.
Vulnerability. *See* Invulnerabiliy.

Wald, George, 27, 28, 130.
Wall, 33, 42.
War: apocalyptic, in nuclear age, 99; automated, 137; effects of, as eternal, 29; excitement of, 30; as festival, 24; in Israelite religion, 94; martyrdom in, 117; meaning of, lost, 40; modern, 33, 38; mythic meaning of, 37–38, 99, 153; opposites united in, 24; as participation in divine power, 95; and peace merge, 44; as

War (*continued*):
play, 79–80; as population control, 114; as ritual, 79–80; as sacred meal, 109–110; as sacrifice, 109, 113; salvation as, 95; as theater, 75–77; traditional view of persists, 48–49; transcendence in, 23; unlimited, appeal of, 24.
Warrior: Americans as, 49–50; as automaton, 137; Canaanite gods as, 93; desires order, 58; everyone as, 100, 103; God as, 93–94, 100; serves death, 24. *See also* Cold warrior.
Wisdom: Bomb possesses, 17; divine, 15; of experts, prestige of, 16; of heroic survivors, 88; of humanity, 45; secret, 15–16, 57. *See also* Omniscience.
Worldview: of cold war, 34–35; of Hiroshima survivors, 123; loss of, and suicide, 129; religion and, 36–37; sacrality of, 38; of strategists, 71.
World War I: dualism in, 33; enemy in, 38; language in, 64, 75; as unending, 28.
World War II: enemy in, 38; J. Glenn Gray's experience in, 22, 24; interpretation of, 3; language in, 76; spectacle in, 76–77; use of Bomb in, 30.